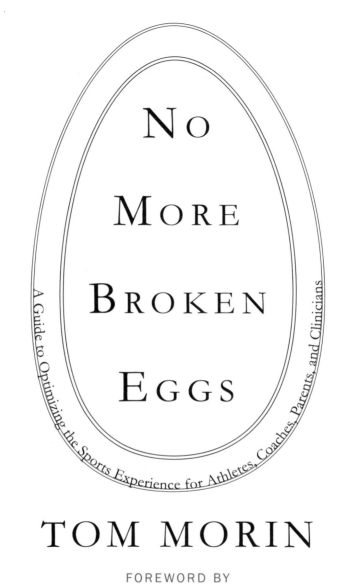

NO

MORE

BROKEN

EGGS

A Guide to Optimizing the Sports Experience for Athletes, Coaches, Parents, and Clinicians

TOM MORIN

FOREWORD BY
MATT BIONDI

INKWATER PRESS

On the cover: Matt Biondi winning the Gold Medal and setting the world record in the 50-meter freestyle at the 1988 Olympic Games in Seoul, Korea. Matt won 11 Olympic medals: eight gold, two silver, and a bronze in the 1984, 1988, and 1992 Olympic Games.

Copyright © 2006 by Tom Morin

Cover and interior design by Masha Shubin

Cover photo © Getty Images. Simon Bruty photographer.

www.inkwaterpress.com

ISBN-10 1-59299-177-7
ISBN-13 978-1-59299-177-8

Publisher: Inkwater Press

Printed in the U.S.A.

To my family,
past, present, and future,
especially
my daughter, Ashton

Table of Contents

Foreword

R eading this book I am reminded of many of my own experiences as an athlete and of the impact my parents and coaches have had on my life. Fortunately for me, my parents saw beyond the excitement of sports to the value for their son in simply participating and getting involved in a variety of activities. As a child I played sports, sang in the choir, and even took piano lessons—which I dreaded. While my mom and dad encouraged me to try different things, they could see that I loved to swim and stood behind my decision to focus on swimming.

From the beginning my mom was there for me, but she didn't let me get too full of myself. When I was ten years old I was playing in the finals of our swim and tennis club's tennis championship. During the match, I threw my racquet and said a few inappropriate things. My mom came down from the stands, grabbed me by the ear, and led me off the court. She drove me home and never said a word about what had happened. Her actions told me that what I did was not appropriate and would not be tolerated. I never acted that way again, and she never brought the situation up again.

My parents didn't expect me to be perfect. I remember when I was in high school we had an away water polo tournament. We were supposed to meet at the school at 5:00 A.M. to catch the team bus to Lodi, which was three hours away. I was so excited about the tournament that I was at the school at 4:30 A.M. When I pulled into the parking lot, mine was the only car there. After a few minutes I started to panic. I guessed that the team must have already left and that I had the time wrong. I quickly drove home, woke up my dad and said "Dad, I missed the team bus to the tournament, can you drive me?" Knowing the tournament was three hours away, without hesitation my dad said, "Let me get a cup of coffee first, then we will go." When I got to the tournament, one of the other guys on the team said "Hey, Matt, where did you go? We saw you pull into the parking lot, then leave." It turns out I had the right time, the bus did leave at 5:00 A.M. A couple guys had already been dropped off and I did not see them waiting under the overhang. Even when my dad found this out, he never complained. This unwavering support was my dad's approach throughout my swimming career.

Fortunately my parents allowed me to make my own decisions. When I was in high school, they were supportive when I decided to quit basketball and play water polo. They knew I loved basketball, but let me make my own decision. Other kids weren't so lucky. I saw many guys over the years who were good at a sport for a few years, then burned out. One kid in particular, I'm sure, could have been a world record holder in swimming. In high school he started skipping practice. He would wet his hair in the sink before his dad picked him up from practice. He was still good enough to sign a full scholarship to a Division One school. He went off to college, but he quit swimming and came home within a year. Along the way in his swimming career the drive to succeed shifted from him to his dad. Because his dad pressured him so much, there was no room for his own drive to continue to develop. Reading the stories of the athletes Tom Morin has worked with and remembering many of the guys I grew up with, I think I can say that when you get down to the core of things, what any athlete wants from his parents is time.

And with the help of a good coach, kids can start to build good work habits and to develop a physical life and not just live from the neck up. At the age of ten I was lucky enough to begin swimming for a coach who was like a pied piper. His name is Stu Kahn. Many of us on the team would show up before practice, just to hang out; we all looked forward to practice. I swam with Stu until I went off to the University of California. Stu had tremendous energy. He made practice fun and exciting. He used to play games or make "deals" with us to get out of practice early. I remember one time Stu bet us he could eat a whole McDonald's hamburger in one bite. When he put the whole hamburger in his mouth, he was not counting on all of us howling with laughter. After all of us started laughing, Stu started to laugh, with the whole hamburger still in his mouth. Without going into details, let's just say Stu didn't win the bet.

When Stu talks about those days now he mentions the support that every child had from his or her parents. When we had a swim meet, no parent dropped his or her child off, and then picked him or her up after the meet. Our swim meets were only three hours long and were often a family affair. These swim meets were short and fun for the whole family. I think that the swim meets today that last from 7:00 A.M. to 7:00 P.M. are unnecessary. Long meets discourage young swimmers from staying in the sport.

The goal of a good coach and the point of Tom's book aren't to create more national records for eight-year-olds. There is no correlation between an eight-year-old national record holder and an Olympian. I knew as an Olympic champion that I was on the pinpoint on the top of a huge pyramid. Coaches need to stop and pay attention to those who do not compete at a high level. They need to help their athletes both to develop life habits like persistence and time management and to learn teamwork and goal setting. In my own experience, I've seen many of my college teammates take what they did in the swimming pool and translate the process into a productive professional career.

As many of the chapters in this book suggest, too much gets lost in the short-term goal of trying to crank out champions. There is a delicate balance that is very important in sports. If a child is forced into an intense situation before he or she has developed the necessary skills, there will be problems. Likewise, if someone has superior skills and is not challenged, he or she becomes stagnant and does not continue to improve.

Of course some things can't be taught. Many of the most successful athletes simply "want success until it burns." From the beginning that is how it was for me. I set a record as a five-year-old that stood for thirty years. I was as nervous as an eight-year-old trying to win a high point trophy as I was before winning an Olympic Gold Medal. By the age of eight I was in my own world before a race. Although I behaved the same way in other sports, I was never as intense as I was when swimming. There is something about swimming that came naturally to me. Swimming felt right. I do not think this can be taught or coached. Many athletes use a word to describe this—"blessed." Fortunately, my parents and coaches gave me enough space to allow this inner drive to grow, develop, and bloom.

Yet I do think it is important for every athlete to have a mentor. To me a mentor is someone you can confide in. Stu Kahn was a mentor for me. In 1976, when I was twelve years old, we all talked about the Olympic Games in Montreal. John Nabor was the swimming star of the 1976 Olympics. Stu said in front of everyone that I was going to be the next John Nabor. It had a tremendous impact on me for someone to believe in me that deeply. I will never forget that moment.

I feel that by the time athletes are ready to go to college, they should know themselves. Athletes should know what type of coach they will work best with. When I went to the University of California, I was on both the swimming and the water polo teams. At Cal I swam for Nort Thornton. Nort's understanding of swimming is off the charts. His office, to this day, is the best swimming library in the country. Nort and I were a good fit. Tom Morin was an assistant coach under Nort. Tom believed in me exactly like Stu Kahn did. By reading this book you will understand why Tom and I worked so well together.

When I played water polo, I played for probably the greatest coach of all time, Pete Cutino. I didn't fully comprehend the benefit of playing for Pete until many years later. Pete was very hard nosed. He was a master of getting you as an athlete to buy into winning the national championship. My freshman year I was scared of Pete. He was a big intimidating guy who yelled often. It was not until my junior and senior year that I saw Pete's friendlier side. He was always demanding, but over the course of four years, I came to understand the method in what I previously thought was madness.

As Tom makes clear in this book, athletes need to be able to look at their strengths and weaknesses. I know one of my former teammates who is a recovering alcoholic. He was able to admit he had a problem and to ask for and get help. Patience, forgiveness, and support are what work for me in my marriage and these same qualities are what will help athletes, parents, and coaches succeed.

Let me end this foreword by speaking as an athlete to other athletes. Do not vacillate from your game. For years Tom Jager was one of my rivals. Tom had the most unorthodox training methods of any athlete ever. One year Tom trained for two weeks, came to the national championships and beat me. Tom was a tenacious competitor. He knew himself really well. At this stage of his career he trusted himself and knew what type of training was best for him.

As an athlete, it only matters what you do. Know what you are good at and stick to it—be confident. I found that the best way to deal with pressure is to know what you have to offer.

Knowing my parents were always there for me gave me tremendous strength and support. At the Olympic Trials one year, I looked over at one of my competitors before the race; he was white as a ghost and looked stiff as a board. He had lost touch with his strengths. He was just scared.

The duality of admitting your weaknesses and knowing your strengths will help you in the long run. Celebrate your strengths. When it is time for a competition, you should have an attitude of "This is what I have; what do you have? I've prepared the best I can; you are going to have to take the win from me." Every athlete should keep in mind when thinking about his or her athletic career to do what it takes to be good for ten years, not by age ten.

– Matt Biondi
April 2006

Introduction

During the 1992 Olympic Games in Barcelona, Spain, Rick DeMont and I went to lunch at a café across from the swimming pool. We originally met in 1981 when I was an assistant swim coach at the University of California, Berkeley, and Rick, in his late twenties, was coming to the end of a long and fascinating swimming career.

Like many children, Rick had asthma. Doctors give the same advice today as they always have given for kids with asthma—join a swim team. Rick excelled in swimming and as a sixteen-year-old, he made the U.S. Olympic team and swam in the 1972 Olympics in Munich, Germany. He qualified for the Olympics in two events, the 400-meter freestyle and the 1500-meter freestyle.

Rick had stated on his medical forms that he took two drugs, Marax and Actifed, for his asthma. At the 1972 Olympic Games, Rick swam the 400-meter freestyle and won the Gold Medal. Two days later he was to swim in the finals of the 1500-meter freestyle, his best event. Rick had set the World Record in the 1500-meter freestyle at the U.S. Olympic Trials. After winning the Gold Medal in the 400-meter freestyle, he was clearly a favorite to win the 1500 as well.

Right before the race it was announced, "The FINA [the international ruling body] has decided to eliminate Rick DeMont, Gold Medal winner over 400-meter freestyle, on the proposal of the Medical Commission of the IOC [International Olympic Committee], from his start over 1500-meters freestyle." Rick was pulled out of the ready room and not allowed to swim the 1500-meter freestyle.

Rick's urine sample taken after the 400-meter freestyle was positive for the banned drug ephedrine. In Rick's urine there were twelve parts per million of ephedrine—without question from his medication. He was stripped of his Gold Medal in the 400 freestyle and did not get a chance to win a second Gold Medal in the 1500 freestyle.

The next year at the World Championships Rick broke the world record in the 400-meter freestyle and became the first person to break the four-minute barrier. He was named Swimmer of the Year in 1973. (For more information on what happened to Rick, go to http://sportsillustrated.cnn.com/olympics/news/2001/01/30/usoc_demont_ap/.)

In 1992 Rick was in Barcelona as Chrissy Ahmann-Leighton's personal swim coach. Chrissy went on to win the Silver Medal in the 100-meter butterfly. I was there as Matt Biondi's personal coach.

What started out as a casual lunch in Barcelona became a turning point in my life. Like many sports, swimming is a world unto itself and those of us in the sport live and breathe swimming. We know all the stories. Those outside of swimming may have heard something about Rick, perhaps not. Terrorists and Mark Spitz's seven Gold Medals overshadowed the Munich Olympics. To those in swimming, what happened to Rick was a tragedy.

Everyone in the world of swimming knew about Rick and what happened to him. Although people know him by name, most would not know him if they saw him. This is typically the case in swimming—names are often known, but often there is not a face to match the name.

At lunch, by chance, we sat at a table with some of the Swedish Olympic swim coaches. It was community seating and we each had our own conversations. After a while we began to talk with the four Swedish coaches. Not knowing who Rick was, one of the coaches asked him "Is the first Olympics you have been to?" Rick replied, "No, I was at Munich too." They asked, "Oh, what's your name?" When he said, "Rick DeMont," all four of them reverently rose in unison to shake his hand. They had a look of awe and admiration on their faces—as if they had met a living legend.

As we began to talk more with the coaches, I congratulated them on the Silver Medal the Swedish team won in the 4 x 200 freestyle relay. In this relay, each of the four swimmers swims a 200-meter freestyle. Sweden won the Silver Medal and the United States finished third with the Bronze Medal. This was quite a triumph for Swedish swimming and was the first time since 1960 the U.S. did not win the Gold Medal.

Sweden's population was about eight million people in 1992. The climate in Sweden is not what one would think of as conducive to producing great swimmers. Here in California, in the Bay Area, age group swimming is great, as California has a more appropriate climate. If we put together an All Star team of twelve-year-olds from the Bay Area, I am confident we could beat the national All Star Team from Sweden. By age twelve we often produce stars but in Sweden twelve-year-olds are just getting started.

However something was happening to these swimmers from the age of about twelve on. How could this small country of Sweden put together four swimmers that could beat the best four swimmers in the United States? When I asked the Swedish coaches this question I got a response I will never forget. They said, "Think of it like a carton of eggs. In the United States you slam all your eggs against the wall and most of them break. In Sweden we can not afford to do that. Our gene pool is too small. We have to bring swimmers along, nurture them while dealing with their setbacks and problems. We have to work with them during the ups and downs of their careers. In the United States, you just get someone else to take his or her place. In Sweden, we have to work on building and developing our swimmers."

I have spoken to parent groups about this conversation many times. I felt what the Swedish coaches said was very true. Here in the United States we are often too focused on how good our kids are in sports by the time they are twelve. We use them, burn them out, and throw them away. We do not do much teaching, nurturing, or instructing; we just try to weed out those that are not the best and we keep pushing and pushing those that are the best to be better. Many young kids never find out how good an athlete they could have been because by the time they are sixteen years old the pressure on them over the years burns them out. They end up being "broken eggs."

Because kids are athletes we often forget that they are still fragile children who need nurturing, instruction, and patience. The goal of this book is to help guide athletes, coaches, parents and clinicians to nurture and work with "eggs," so they don't end up broken. Many of the athletes I talk about could have ended up "broken eggs" and two actually did. I will talk about my work as both a coach and a psychotherapist working in the field of Sport Psychology. I will show how many of the athletes I worked with were very close to getting out of sports for one reason or another. I hope this book can guide some of those who are on the edge to figure out how to perform better in sports in general and over the long haul reach higher peaks than would otherwise have been attainable.

Here in the United States we run far too many kids out of sports before we ever really know what they could have done. One of my basic beliefs is that the benefits from a successful sports experience last a lifetime. Through sports, kids can learn the lessons of life. This only happens if they are active in sports.

James Michener wrote in his book *The Bridge at Andau*, "For any nation to deprive itself of the capacities of any man is really a sin against the entire society. And if a system not only refuses to use native capacities but establishes a regime for stunting or destroying those capacities, then such a regime is doomed."* Michener was talking about the horrible impact that communism had on the people of Hungary, leading to the 1956 revolt against their Russian oppressors.

The way our youth sport programs stunt and destroy many of our young and developing "eggs" is a sin against our society. It is time to stop and take a hard look at the structure of youth sport programs in the United States and the impact they are having on our children. It is clear that we are destroying far too many of our precious "eggs."

❂   ❂   ❂   ❂

It was not until January of 2003, while I was part of a Sport Psychology seminar, that I began to contemplate writing a book about how to nurture our young athletes. Hosted at John F. Kennedy University in the San Francisco Bay Area, where I teach graduate school, the seminar was designed for those working in the field of Sport Psychology.

This was a one-day seminar and there were three different panels. Each person on the panel spoke for about ten minutes, followed by a question-and-answer session. The first panel, the one I was on, consisted of four people. The main speaker was Tom Tutko, Ph.D., known to many as The Father of Sport Psychology. The second panel was made up of successful local coaches from different sports. The third panel consisted of athletes from professional, college, and high school sports.

Many in the audience were current or former graduate stu-

---

* Michener, James A. *The Bridge at Andau*. New York: Random House, Inc., 1957

dents of mine. These people understand that the mental side of sports is incredibly important. They wanted to hear more about the work that each of us on the panel was doing. We each talked in our own way about what we saw as important issues focusing on the mental (not physical) side of sports preparation. We included case studies where our work with athletes had been successful. Because the audience was primarily made up of those that either had studied, or were studying Sport Psychology, we were preaching to the choir, so to speak.

The genesis of this book came from the coaches' panel. Although there were six coaches on the second panel, none of the coaches came to hear the first panel. The seminar took place on a Saturday, and of course there were the expected calendar conflicts due to practices. However, if any member was interesting in learning something new, one would expect him or her to have attended the first panel with the famous Tom Tutko. The same format was used for the second panel. Each coach spoke for about ten minutes, with a question-and-answer session following.

Each coach spoke of the importance of the mental side of sports. A primary topic dealt with the pressures and emotional issues their athletes had encountered. Most said they had tried to foster a winning attitude. However, during the question-and-answer session, the exchange between the coaches and the audience turned hostile. The coaches were saying that while "Sport Psychology is important, I don't need anyone else's help—it is something I do as a coach." One coach said, "In all my years of coaching, I have never had an athlete that I felt needed a Sport Psychologist." This was a coach who worked with many young women, in a sport known for eating disorders. The coaches' attitude reminded me of Mark Twain's saying that if all you know how to do is hammer—everything looks like a nail. All these coaches knew how to do was focus on the physical performance of their athletes. They clearly did not take the same type of nurturing approach toward their athletes as the Swedish coaches did. I felt that the coaches on this panel were likely to be "egg smashers."

With my coaching background, I could understand how coaches would be protective of their athletes and their coaching style. I was very protective of the athletes I coached, and did not want anyone coming near them unless they had something substantial to offer. However, there were people who did have something to offer. For me to deny my athletes' access to someone that could help them with nutrition, stretching, weight lifting or anything else would have been detrimental to their careers.

When I was coaching at the University of California, we would have athletes work with a strength coach for their weight lifting. We would bring in a nutritionist to do a lecture about proper diet for college athletes. A yoga instructor would come in and help us with stretching. Trainers would work with injured athletes on determining the best course of rehabilitation. And of course we had Sport Psychologists come in and talk to the team about Sport Psychology. As coaches, we knew we did not have the answers to everything and were always open to someone who had something to offer.

The coaches at the conference seemed to be closed minded, saying, "I can take care of all of my athlete's psychological needs." Many of these coaches had experience but little if any education or training in the psychological aspects of sport. Their experience was limited to their coaching or personal playing experience, rather than experience working with athletes in a clinical setting on sport-related issues. These coaches saw the physical preparation side of sports and tended to ignore the mental side of athletic performance, apart from fostering a "winning attitude." They believed athletes need to be mentally tough, but did not seem to grasp that mental toughness comes from self-confidence. Focusing on mental toughness before focusing on self-confidence is like trying to teach children to run before they can walk.

I also had to wonder if these coaches felt fully prepared to help an athlete who has a verbally abusive, alcoholic parent. Did they have any idea the impact on someone's self-esteem this kind of parent can have? Did they feel qualified to work with an athlete with an eating disorder? How could they help athletes who felt their coach was the source of their problems? Would they know how to handle athletes who have parents who are constantly pressuring their children to succeed? How would they deal with a college athlete who has a very ill or dying parent or grandparent, or relationship problems? Could they help an athlete with a drug or alcohol problem? Did they take into consideration the psychological issues that come into play when an athlete is recovering from a serious injury? Were these coaches aware of the psychological impact on an athlete whose parents are going through a divorce? How would they work with an athlete who thinks he or she chokes in pressure situations? Could they give an athlete unbiased advice if an athlete wanted to transfer to another coach or school, or even quit the sport?

Here we are in Northern California, probably one of the most therapy friendly areas of the country, and encountering this type of attitude surprised me. I walked out of that seminar and thought to myself, "I have to sort out these important issues and I have to find the answers." In writing and researching this book, the feeling for me was not "I want to" but "I have to."

I am an educator. As a coach teaching was my primary role. It is my hope that this book helps to guide and educate the reader so everyone can get the most out of his or her sports experience. The personal and psychological results from a good sports experience last a lifetime. Too often parents and coaches like the ones on the panel can be the ones who end up destroying the "eggs." I hope that the stories in this book will help show readers the importance of nurturing our young athletes, helping them through their problems, and optimizing both their sports experience and their future lives.

NO MORE BROKEN EGGS

CHAPTER 1

Kathy—A College Diver

Kathy, a senior in college and a member of the diving team, was referred to me by her coach. He was at the end of his rope. He did not know what to do and turned to me for help. Right before the NCAA Championships during each of her first three years Kathy had had an accident. Typically she'd hit her arm on the board, break a bone, and be unable to compete in the championships.

The coach described Kathy as a very talented diver. Like many divers she was a former gymnast and was incredibly athletic. He said she was a head case when it came to big competition (eleven dives in a competition) and that many of her best performances were in competitions that meant little. He indicated to me that I was his last hope.

This was the beginning of her senior year and he did not want to work with her all year only to have her college career end with another accident. During the course of the time I worked with Kathy I had little, if any, contact with her coach. He knew and trusted me and he allowed me complete therapy flexibility.

Think of a car with a flat tire. It's not the end of the world, but it is an inconvenience. However, if the tire falls off—that's another story. If all four tires fall off, transportation reaches a whole new level. By way of illustration, if the car then catches on fire too…. Too often it takes a "totaled car, on fire" for a coach to look for psychological help for their athletes. Coaches try to handle the problem themselves—but are often unaware that they are ill-equipped to solve these problems. Sometimes, they blame the athletes, or try to replace them. Fortunately for everyone, Kathy's coach did not throw this "egg" out. He sought help.

In this instance the coach truly liked Kathy and wanted her to succeed. For the sake of both of them he was willing to do anything. He told me, when referring her to me, "I will do anything you say—I don't know what to do anymore. I've tried everything."

How did Kathy feel about being sent to see me? She also wanted help and her attitude seemed quite good. She said, "I don't know why I have had those accidents, but I don't want the same thing to happen this year—for my sake, my coach and my team."

Before we began our work I asked for some background information. Kathy told me that she began diving seriously in high school and was going along just fine until the Junior National Championships of her senior year. During the warm-ups for the first day's competition she had an incident.

A reverse dive is a dive in which the diver leaves the board, jumps straight up, pulls her knees into her chest and flips or spins backward, with the back of her head passing close to the board. Reverse dives are dangerous dives. Greg Louganis hit his head on the diving board while attempting a reverse dive during the 1988 Olympics. Also, Louganis was one of the few divers to do a reverse three and a half somersault from the ten-meter platform. The reverse three and a half is known as "the dive of death," after a Russian diver died after hitting his head on the platform while attempting the dive.

During the three-meter competition Kathy was doing her last warm-up for a reverse dive and she came very close to the board. Her ponytail actually hit the board and this terrified her. When she got up to do her next reverse she balked, which is when a diver comes to the end of the board and stops, does not do the dive, and either jumps or just falls in the water. To balk at the Junior National Championships is very embarrassing. Her coach then yelled at her in front of everyone. This brought her to tears and the rest of the three-meter competition was horrible for her.

The next day during warm-up for the ten-meter platform competition her confidence was clearly shaken. She was very tentative during her first few warm-up dives. On about her fourth warm-up dive she landed flat on her back. To anyone who has been around diving, this is a familiar "splat" sound and everyone turns to see who did it and if they are all right. She came to the side of the pool to talk with her coach and said she did not want to do any more warm-up dives. Her coach was from the school of "When you fall off the horse—you get right back on." He told her to go up and do the same dive again.

By the time she climbed the ten-meter tower she was in tears; she was in no condition to continue. She seemed to regain her composure and attempted the dive. She was in a forward tuck and did not kick out of the tuck. She hit the water still spinning and in a ball, and her face hit the water first. Kathy was almost unconscious and bleeding from her eyes and had to be helped from the water. Everyone gathered around her to see if she was okay. Paramedics came and Kathy was taken to the emergency room to assure that she was not seriously injured.

When incidents like this happen it is easy to have anyone, especially an athlete, take it very personally. Not many people knew who she was—they just knew someone had an accident. In sports, they become known as "that girl" or "that guy." Kathy was now "that girl who was taken to the hospital bleeding from her eyes." There was no physical damage from the accident but she did not compete again in the Junior Nationals.

Athletes feel a tremendous sense of shame and embarrassment from accidents like the one Kathy experienced. They feel like everyone knows what happened to them. They begin to question their ability to perform at any level. Self-doubt is like a cancer that takes hold of an athlete and will continue to grow unless treated. Like all people with serious problems, athletes' and coaches' first response is to ignore these problems and hope the athletes cure themselves. They use the defense mechanism of denial and try to deny the impact of what has happened. They mistakenly think they need to put an incident like this behind them and end up ignoring the issue.

Self-doubt is like a cancer that takes hold of an athlete and will continue to grow unless treated. Like all people with serious problems, athletes' and coaches' first response is to ignore these problems and hope the athletes cure themselves. They use the defense mechanism of denial and try to deny the impact of what has happened. They mistakenly think they need to put an incident like this behind them and end up ignoring the issue.

Thus, a common problem when something like this happens at the end of the season is to try to move on. Both athletes and coaches think this is what they need to do; they rationalize, thinking that after all, it is over and done with—why dwell on it? Often the problem does disappear—until the same situation comes up again, usually about a year later at the same level of competition.

This background information was very important as we got started. The next important piece of information was that in her three years of collegiate diving, Kathy had *never* done a reverse two and a half dive in practice, even though she attempted these dives everyday. Although she was able to do a reverse double (two somersaults) from the one and a half–meter board, she was not able to do a reverse two and a half from the three-meter board. She would balk every single time!

She stated that she was able to do the reverse two and a half from the three-meter board in competition. She said she never did very well on it but usually scored fives on the dive. Dives are scored on a scale from one to ten. There are a number of judges and a diver may get a score of five from one judge and five and a half from another, etc.

I knew that attempting to do this dive daily was not good at all psychologically. I told Kathy that I had decided she was not allowed to attempt this dive in practice for at least two weeks. I did this during our first session during the month of September. She did not have any real competitions for a while as her championships were not until March. I knew the way things had been going up until now was not working at all. I knew it had to be horrible for her self-esteem to daily remind herself that she was a failure by attempting and not completing the dive. I knew that I had to do something right away.

When the pressure was off an interesting thing happened. Her other dives began to improve! In the past much of her practice time was spent getting ready to try her reverse two and a half. Now she could focus on her other dives without the reverse two and a half looming in the background. With the mental pressure off, her self-confidence began to grow.

After the two weeks went by I extended my ban on the reverse two and a half for two more weeks. I knew if Kathy really wanted to do this dive, or felt she could do it, she would do it no matter what I said, but she seemed perfectly happy not to do the dive. During the second two-week ban she did have a competition and once again did the dive for fives. However in the competition all her other dives were much better. Whereas in the past when she would get sixes and six and a halfs, she began to get sevens and seven and a halfs. That was a huge improvement!

Kathy finally placed higher than the diver who had consistently beaten her in college did, and both she and her coach were pleased with her results. Her confidence and self-esteem continued to grow. We were trying to change how she saw herself. Instead of the image of a bad diver who can't do a reverse two and a half; she began to see herself as a good diver who can't do one particular dive. Although this may seem obvious to an outsider, Kathy did not appreciate this perspective prior to our working together.

During that first month she was still practicing the reverse one and half and prepping the two and a half by doing reverse double somersaults, all done on the one and a half meter–board. She was also practicing the reverse two and a half in the belts. Divers often train on a pit of foam rubber where they are harnessed in belts attached to ropes. The ropes are attached to a pulley and the coach holds the end of the rope. This is dry land training for divers. The diver dives off a diving board into the foam pit and as they do the dive, the coach spots them with the ropes. He pulls on the ropes as the diver completes the dive to elevate the belt they are wearing, and the diver lands gently on the foam. Thus, much of the risk of injury is eliminated. Kathy was practicing the reverse two and a half in the belts with the coach spotting her. She would also practice these dives on a trampoline.

After a month I felt it was time for her to attempt a reverse two and a half in practice and I told her to pick one day during the week and on that day she would make one attempt at the dive. If she did it, fine. If she balked, she was not allowed to try the dive again that week. Once again, I did not want her to go back to feeling like a failure. This went on for about three weeks and she never did the dive in practice. She balked every time, but it did not impact her as much. She was able to move on to her other dives, which were still improving.

We began to work on visualization. Many athletes at Kathy's level can visualize on their own, without instruction. She tried to avoid the reverse two and a half all together, even when she visualized. So we began by having Kathy starting to visualize doing the dive successfully. This included how her approach should look and feel, how her jump should feel, how she should feel in the air and on her entry into the water. I had her work at visualization both at home and in the belts just before she did the dive. After a short time doing this, she began to see herself doing the dive successfully.

I also asked her to explain to me how the dive should be performed. I did this so she would not only be able to visualize the dive, but also be able to articulate how it should work. I felt that if she could get me to understand the process of how the dive should be done properly, then she would understand how the dive should be done as well. In other words, by getting her to explain the dive to me, she had to sort it out in her head and understand the dive completely and all its nuances.

She said that after her jump, as she was spinning backwards, she should see the sky, then the water, then the sky again then the water again then the sky, then she should kick. First of all, this amazed me! I could not imagine processing this information in this short time span because I didn't even know that divers had their eyes open! But in doing two and half revolutions it made sense: She would have to see the sky three times and the water twice! As this became clearer to me it became clearer to her too as well!

She began to see the dive as a manageable task and began to see herself doing the dive successfully. She had the kinesthetic feel of the dive from her work in the belts and prepping on the low board. At the same time her self-confidence was constantly growing and her diving was improving. However this brought up a new set of problems.

As she began to get better, she began to win competitions, which brought up issues from the past. Her sister had been a senior in high school when Kathy was a freshman. Her sister was also a diver, but she was neither as good nor as talented as Kathy was. During one competition toward the end of the season Kathy was ahead of her sister. They were the top two divers going into the last round of dives. Kathy's mom was at the competition. She came over to Kathy before her last dive and said, "Why don't you let your sister win this one, it will make the ride home easier for all of us." Interestingly enough, the last dive she was to throw was a reverse dive.

Earlier in our sessions Kathy had said something to me like "I've always had trouble with reverses" and she explained that jumping off the board and spinning backwards had been a problem for her. It sure made sense to me but now I began to wonder if her problem with reverses might have had other causes as well.

Kathy missed her last dive and let her sister win. Afterward her mom thanked her and told her that after all, her sister was a senior, and she was a freshman and she would have many chances to win competitions. However as Kathy began to get better during our time together and began to win, she felt bad for the girls she was beating.

Many of these girls had beaten Kathy for all three years of college and now she was beating them. She began to wonder if her winning was hurting the other girls' feelings and what their moms were saying to them. I explained to her that although her mom's intentions were good, what she did was wrong. Her sister never knew, and I doubted she would have wanted to win by Kathy's throwing the competition. Also I pointed out that this could be where the hesitation on the reverse dives started because she had begun a pattern of being tentative on this dive and blew it to let her sister win.

Kathy was an art student and her diving was her form of artistic self-expression. We focused on her own expression and not what the other artist/divers were doing. They may have had their own critics—parents/coaches—but she needed to express her art and keep the focus on her. We focused on how things should feel and that we needed to help things flow during the competition.

As the season progressed Kathy's diving soared and she was now getting eights, eight and a halfs, and even an occasional nine. Her reverse two and a half was getting better but it was still her weakest dive, usually earning only fives and sixes. The most encouraging thing was that her self-esteem was growing. As we approached the end of the season I knew we needed to talk about the accidents of the past three years.

Kathy did not really want to look back at these accidents. When I explained that we needed to do this to help ensure against a reoccurrence, she was more receptive. As she talked about these accidents it became clear to both of us that her family history was inextricably tied to the incident at the Junior Nationals her senior year in high school.

Clinically, one way to look at what happened at the Junior Nationals was to view it as a trauma. She was overwhelmed with anxiety because of the upcoming big competition, and now each time it came close to a chance for the earlier trauma to repeat itself she unconsciously did something—get hurt—to prevent the trauma from recurring. This was her way of unconsciously dealing with her anxiety, her trauma. By having an accident she removed herself from the chance of re-experiencing her big hurt.

I felt we needed to go back to the original incident, even though it was four years ago, to get some resolution. We did this in depth for a couple sessions and she processed what had happened. I had her take me step by step through exactly what happened and we talked about her thoughts, feelings, and emotions associated with this incident.

She began to see that since her senior year of high school she had picked up some faulty thought patterns and after this incident her own self-talk turned negative. Because of the trauma at the Junior Nationals she saw herself as a choke artist and someone who could not handle the pressure of a big competition. The accidents in each of the past three years reinforced this opinion of herself.

I knew it was critically important to reframe what had happened and her view of herself. If we went into the end of the season with the same mindset, there would be another accident. I got her to see that all along she had been a very good diver, who had a bad experience at the Junior Nationals, but this did not negate the successes she had experienced up until that competition. During the past three years, she had great successes and was obviously a talented diver. She began to see that the accidents of the past three years were simply that—accidents. It was important to incorporate this self-conception of competence in her mind. She had to see herself as a good diver who had a few bad dives and that this was natural and common to all sports.

Things were going fine right up to the conference championships but she was still not doing the reverse two and a half in practice even though she was able to do it in the belts and in competition. She talked about her nerves leading up to the conference championships and we were able to work on some breathing and relaxation. This came very easy for her as she was not a high-strung person to start with.

We also rehearsed the competition, which was to take place at a complex where she had competed many times. We went over all the senses she would experience including what the pool smelled like, an easy one because they all smell to some extent of chlorine. We went over what the ladder and the diving board felt like under her feet and the sounds she would be hearing. We went over details like where she would go between dives and what music she would listen to with her headphones. By going into as much detail as possible we took out any surprises from the competition. The goal was that by the time she was there she would be relaxed and everything would seem familiar.

The conference championship was a success; she placed very high and qualified to compete in the NCAA Championships two weeks later. Once again we worked on staying calm and relaxing. Many coaches talk about giving 110%, which often leads to athletes trying too hard. They get so tense and nervous that things do not flow for them. I knew that we had to work to keep Kathy relaxed at the NCAA Championships.

> She had to see herself as a good diver who had a few bad dives and that this was natural and common to all sports.

It was important in the two weeks leading up to the NCAAs to keep focusing on her breathing, relaxation, and visualization. Once again I reassured her that she did not need to do the reverse two and a half in practice as she had not done one all year (actually four years). She was able to do the dive for a score of six and a half at the conference meet. It was her worst dive, of course, but she had eights or higher on many of her other dives. After the conference meet she was really able to see that she was not a bad diver but a very good diver with just one weak dive.

The NCAAs were a great experience for her and she was able to do the reverse two and a half for sevens and her other dives were once again great. She made the finals while competing against some of the best divers in the world. Both she and her coach were very proud of how she did at the NCAA Championships and throughout her senior year.

Kathy's senior year ended on a great note and she was able to finish her diving career with a positive attitude and a healthy self-esteem. Kathy could have easily ended up a "broken egg." Instead she learned a valuable life lesson.

CHAPTER 2

Ernie—A Baseball Star Dealing With Injuries

At some point in their careers many athletes have to deal with injuries. Most athletes do not make good patients. The same drive and determination that makes athletes successful also makes them impatient patients. Athletes can easily set season-long goals in their sport, but when it comes to an injury they want to be back competing as soon as possible. They often fail to set goals along the way in the rehabilitation process. This rush to rehab causes many problems. Athletes often re-injure themselves trying to come back too soon. In some cases, careers end because of a lack of patience during the rehab process.

In high school, Ernie was known as a "phenom" (short for phenomenon). Phenoms are athletes who come along every once in a while and are far better than their peers. Ernie is a baseball player. While in high school, Ernie led the league in every hitting category. He had the most runs batted in (RBIs), best batting average (around .600), most doubles, triples, and home runs. He was named MVP (most valuable player) for his league and was one of the top prospects coming out of high school in California. Everyone figured Ernie was a future professional baseball star. He was constantly compared to professional baseball players.

While in high school, Ernie focused solely on baseball. Some baseball players go straight from high school to professional baseball's minor leagues. They never go to college. Other players may play a year or two of college baseball, and then move on to professional baseball. And some players play all four years of college, then go on to professional baseball.

Ernie did not study much in high school because baseball was his whole life. His grades were just good enough for him to remain eligible, nothing more. He was drafted by a professional team out of high school, but decided to sign with a Division One school to play college baseball. He thought a year or two of college baseball could help him get to the big leagues faster. Academics had no role in his college choice.

Toward the end of Ernie's senior year of high school, once baseball season was over, he rarely went to class. He found out a couple days before graduation that he was going to fail a class and would not be able to participate in the school's graduation ceremonies. In the past, many teachers simply passed Ernie, knowing his future was in baseball, not in the classroom. This time around, Ernie was faced with a different situation. Since he would not graduate from high school, he automatically was not eligible to go on to college. Thus, he automatically forfeited his scholarship and his chance, for now, to play Division One baseball. That same week Sarah, his girlfriend, dumped him. She was a year behind him in school and wanted the option of dating other guys her senior year. A few days later Ernie went to the doctor to have his knee checked. The doctor told Ernie that he had a torn ligament and needed surgery before he could play baseball again. Knee surgery removed the option of going to play in the minor leagues.

Ernie's world had been turned upside down; it would take him another four years and much soul searching before he decided he might need some counseling. Athletes often feel they should be able to handle their own problems. Unfortunately, they often view going to a counselor as a sign of weakness. Because their past success has been of their own doing, they feel they can get themselves out of any problem—no matter how complex or severe the problem is. This belief in their self-sufficiency ends the careers of many athletes. Since athletes would rather fix their own problems than appear weak, they get no help. Their own beliefs destroy them.

Before Ernie came to see me, he was completely overwhelmed and knew he needed help. When I first saw Ernie he was twenty-two years old and was not sure what to do with his life. Some of his high school teammates were already playing Major League Baseball. Ernie felt he was at a critical crossroads in his life.

After high school Ernie was disoriented and confused. He decided to take some time off after his knee surgery to try to figure out what he should do. He eventually ended up passing the class he failed and graduating from high school. After a very brief rehab process from the knee surgery, Ernie enrolled at a local community college to play baseball. The community college team was not Division One baseball, but it was still baseball and that was good enough for Ernie. During the preseason, Ernie hurt his ankle. He still tried to play through the pain, but soon realized he needed to see a doctor. When the doctor told Ernie he would need another surgery, Ernie was shocked. Ankle surgery is much more complex than knee surgery. The doctor told Ernie it would take at least three months before he could even walk on his own again.

Ernie rushed through the rehab process after his knee surgery, making his ankle more vulnerable to injury. Since his identity was solely dependent on baseball, Ernie's only focus during the rehab process from knee surgery was to get back on the field and play again. Had he followed the recommended course of action during the rehab process, he probably would not have injured his ankle.

Over the next five years, Ernie had four different surgeries and never played college baseball at all. After each surgery, he was depressed, confused, and distraught; all he would do was try to go back to playing baseball as soon as he could. Ernie never allowed himself to heal. Each surgery was the result of being an impatient patient, and the mistaken belief that he should be able to play through pain.

When we first met, Ernie reported to me the events of late. Although he had not played college baseball, he did participate in a semi-pro summer league the previous summer. It was the first time Ernie had played organized baseball since high school. He played in a Wooden Bat League, a league for former college players who still loved to play baseball. Some of the players were hoping to get drafted into the Minor Leagues. Incredibly, even after not playing since high school, Ernie led the league in hitting. His batting average was .539. This means Ernie was getting a hit in 53.9% of his at-bats. He was named MVP of the league.

I have always been fascinated by baseball. A professional player can fail to get a hit 70% of the time and still be very successful. A player's batting average is based on the number of hits he gets for each at-bat. Walks are not factored into the batting average. Walks are factored into on base percentage, the number of times a batter reaches base for each at-bat. If a player starts the season getting three hits in three at-bats—he is batting 1000. If another player goes zero hits for three at-bats—his batting average is 000. Ted Williams is the last professional player to hit over .400 for a season (.406 in 1941), which means even Ted Williams failed to get a hit almost 60% of the time. To keep a positive attitude under such circumstances seems hard.

Ernie was frustrated. He felt nothing he did in the Wooden Bat League was good enough. Since he was not playing Major League Baseball, he felt like a failure. One reason Ernie came to see me was because he had to make a decision regarding surgery again. The same ankle injury he had out of high school was now back. Ernie did not know if, at the age of twenty-two, he should have surgery again or not. He thought it might be time to give up on his baseball dreams. He knew that if he had the ankle surgery it would mean three to four weeks on crutches and about four weeks in a walking boot. Once the boot was removed, he would have to walk with a cane for a few weeks until he could finally walk on his own. We met in late July. Ernie had already scheduled the surgery, but was not sure whether to proceed or not.

One interesting thing that had changed dramatically in Ernie's life was his approach to his education. Ernie was now a junior honors student at the University of California, Berkeley. Cal, as locals call it, is one of the top academic schools in the country. In the years since high school, Ernie started to apply himself in the classroom. He realized that he might not be able to make a living playing baseball, so he began to study. He was shocked to find out that he could succeed in the classroom. He used to think some kids were just naturally smart. He started to see his performance in the classroom much like his performance in baseball. When he did the assigned work in school, good results followed. Ernie realized being smart was an exercise in persistence. I tell my college students "Education is a measure of persistence—not intelligence."

I am a firm believer in having options. I explained to Ernie that if he went through with the surgery, he could possibly have the option of returning to baseball. Without the surgery, baseball was not an option for him at all. Ernie had done his research and found a doctor who had performed the same type of surgery on professional athletes. Ernie was confident that he found the right doctor. However, he was not confident in his ability to come back from surgery.

Many athletes often have a myopic view when it comes to sports. They are able to focus on a single game or even a whole season, but often are unable to take a long-term view of their whole career. I pointed out to Ernie that many professional baseball players are in their thirties. Although some of the kids he played with and against in high school were already in the Major Leagues, other baseball players take years to make it to the Majors. I stressed that for Ernie the big picture could mean he might not be in the Major Leagues for a few years. Without the surgery there was no big picture for him that included baseball.

Ernie was still very confused about his identity. I often see identity problems with athletes when their careers are over. Ernie was known as a baseball player—that's it. Because of his success in baseball he was one of the popular kids in high school. Part of Ernie's confusion was that he felt like he was trying to recapture his high school glory days.

Interestingly enough, Ernie was still obsessed with Sarah—his high school girlfriend who dumped him five years ago. He felt like if he could succeed in baseball again, somehow the success would bring Sarah back to him. Sarah, baseball, and his high school popularity were all linked together in his mind; they were the reasons why he always hurried through the rehab process after the previous surgeries.

Ernie had always been a shy person. In the past, baseball helped him socially in many ways. Without baseball in his life the past five years, his social life was nonexistent. In fact, he could now be diagnosed with social phobia. Social phobia is when a person fears being embarrassed in public. The social phobic person avoids public situations, rarely talks to others, and has a disorder that is much more severe than being shy.

Ernie told me he had been dating one of his former college teachers. While at another school, at the end of the semester, one of his teachers asked him out. Ernie had rarely spoken to a woman in the past few years. He had not dated anyone since Sarah dumped him. When he was dating his teacher he was not happy, but he did not want to break up with her because of the pain he felt when Sarah dumped him. Ernie ended up doing things so the teacher finally broke up with him, much to his relief. It was obvious Ernie did not know how to express his feelings in any situation.

Early in our work together, Ernie brought up his anxiety. He said that even though he hit over .500 in the Wooden Bat League, he still experienced butterflies in his stomach. He was anxious before every at-bat. He was also anxious with women. If he was out with his friends and a girl showed she was interested in Ernie, he would freeze up and not respond at all. His self-confidence was so low that if a woman smiled at him, Ernie would turn around and look behind him to see whom she was smiling at—he felt like there was no way she was smiling at him. Furthermore, Ernie still only hung out with former high school friends. He had not made any new friends in the past five years. Ernie said he did not talk much when out with his friends. He never even told his friends that he was going to school at Berkeley. Ernie could best be described as a wallflower, someone who is just there.

From the beginning of our work together, I knew I needed to address Ernie's self-confidence. I knew that regardless of his ankle, for him to succeed, his confidence in himself needed to improve drastically. Ernie was terribly afraid of making mistakes. Before batting, he feared striking out or somehow being embarrassed. In dealing with women, he feared he would "say the wrong thing and look stupid." I decided to start with the easiest task first. I suggested to Ernie that he approach talking with women the same way he approached batting practice. I told him that the next time he was out with his friends, I wanted him to find a girl he was not interested in at all, approach her, and talk briefly with her. He was to use the conversation with the girl as practice. I wanted to remove the self-imposed pressure that Ernie felt. By taking the pressure off the conversation with a woman, I felt he would relax. More times than not, an issue affects all areas of a person's life. In this case, Ernie's anxiety, fear, and self-imposed pressure affected all areas of his life. Many people tell athletes to just relax. Relaxing is not a simple task. I wanted to teach Ernie how to relax. To relax, it is imperative to remove the self-imposed pressure. With any new skill, it is important to practice the skill in a low-pressure situation. Even thinking about talking to a woman whom he is not interested in still caused anxiety for Ernie.

Ernie decided to have the surgery on his ankle. While he was on crutches and in a walking cast I had time to address some of the deeper issues I knew Ernie needed to resolve in order to succeed.

In our next few sessions, while he was on crutches, Ernie kept talking about his previous relationship with Sarah. Now that Ernie was using his brain much more, he often spent time over-analyzing situations. Somehow, Ernie came to believe that succeeding in baseball was not his destiny. Like many baseball players, Ernie was superstitious. He thought, "If I was meant to succeed, I would have succeeded by now." I did not feel Ernie had taken enough personal responsibility during his past rehabilitation processes. He often had not followed the physical therapist's or doctor's recommendations, thinking, "If I want it bad enough, I should be able to play." I pointed out to him that his body was made to play baseball. He looked like a baseball player. He clearly had incredible athletic ability. I told him if he could be more patient with himself, I was confident he could succeed in baseball. I said I did not know if he could play professional baseball, but if he carefully allowed his body to heal properly, he could have the opportunity to find out how far he could go in baseball. I stressed something had to be different this time around during the rehabilitation process.

Ernie also over-analyzed his previous relationship with Sarah. He felt like his relationship with Sarah was a dividing line in his life. He saw every experience in his life after Sarah broke up with him as bad. His life before the break-up, he saw as good. I tried to reframe his view of this dividing line. I explained to Ernie that I saw the break-up as a line of change—because of all the changes he had gone through since the break-up. I told him that many of the changes were obviously for the better. Prior to the break-up he was a below-average student; I reminded him of the academic success he had since the break-up. In high school, Ernie struggled as a student. Now, he was now an honor student at one of the best academic institutions in the country. He was well read and enjoyed writing. I told him that the turn of events at the end of his senior year might end up being the best thing that ever happened to him.

One thing I kept stressing to Ernie as he was beginning the rehab process was to be patient with himself. I told him the biggest mistake he could make was to try once again to come back too soon. Ernie felt that if he could get back to playing baseball successfully, somehow the success in baseball would bring him personal happiness and Sarah back into his life. Patience is a virtue many athletes do not possess while undergoing rehabilitation. I knew for Ernie to succeed he had to learn how to be patient with himself. Ernie needed to learn how to listen to his body. In the past his mind told him he should be able to play through pain. The pain Ernie felt was his body's way of signaling he was not ready to play. To heal properly, Ernie needed to learn how to listen to his body instead of his mind.

As we continued to meet, Ernie began to show signs of improvement. His dilemma now was which school to play baseball for. Should he try to play for the University of California, or play for one of the local community colleges? The quandary Ernie faced was how to approach and talk with the college coaches. Being social phobic, Ernie was terrified of going in and talking with the Cal baseball coaches. He knew one of the assistant coaches at one of the local community colleges and felt comfortable talking with him. The community college coach, who knew Ernie from his high school days, said as long as Ernie signed up for classes for the Spring semester, he could play for their team. Cal, on the other hand is a Division One baseball program. I knew if Ernie walked into the Cal coach's office and told the coach his statistics, the coach would leap at the opportunity of having Ernie play for Cal. Although I saw the situation this way, Ernie did not. Ernie was scared the Cal coach would see him on crutches and want nothing to do with him. Also, he felt that he would be a burden to the coach and would interrupt the coach. Since he was so terrified about talking with the coach, Ernie sent the coach an e-mail. Every college coach has students who approach him or her who want to try out for their team. Most of these students have no chance of making a Division One college team. I knew Ernie was different. If the coach simply looked at Ernie, listened to his statistics, and talked with him for five minutes, the coach would want Ernie to come and at least try out for the team.

Ernie decided that when he was out of his walking cast he would approach the Cal coach. In a situation like this, I have to work to control my impulses. I wanted to call the Cal coach and tell him about Ernie. However, I felt that if Ernie's confidence in himself was to improve, he needed to contact the coach on his own. I did mention to Ernie that I would soon see John Hughes, a friend of mine who is a professional baseball scout. I asked Ernie if he wanted me to ask John for his advice about which school to play for—Cal or a community college. Ernie felt like if he played for a community college he would get much more playing time; with Cal he was not sure about the amount of playing time he would get. Ernie seemed excited and asked me to go ahead and speak with John.

When I explained the situation to John, he was very interested. John told me that while playing at either school, Ernie would be seen by professional baseball scouts. He pointed out that playing at Cal would carry more weight with the scouts. However, John said the amount of playing time Ernie would get was an important factor in deciding which school to play for. John knew one of the Cal assistant coaches, gave me his name, and said to have Ernie contact the coach and say John suggested that Ernie contact him. John also stressed the importance of being healthy. He did point out that since Ernie would not be healthy until January, playing at a community college might be the better choice. The college baseball season starts at the end of January.

As Ernie and I continued to meet, I began to notice a difference in him. Ernie was making more eye contact with me during our sessions. For someone who is social phobic, speaking to a therapist can be overwhelming. I took Ernie's increased eye contact with me as a sign that his self-confidence was improving. In chemical dependency treatment and in dealing with athletes I often use the phrase "fake it till you make it." I suggested Ernie fake it till he makes it as far as his self-confidence. I told him for now, just to pretend he was confident, that pretending was all he needed to do now. Ernie told me that he approached a woman at a bar whom he was not interested in and started a conversation with her. Her boyfriend was in the band at the bar and her friends had not yet arrived, so she was glad to have someone to talk to. Soon some of her friends came and Ernie ended up

> In chemical dependency treatment and in dealing with athletes I often use the phrase "fake it till you make it."

dancing with one of the girl's friends. Ernie had not danced in a long time. I knew that Ernie had taken a step in the right direction to help him deal with his anxiety.

Ernie began to talk more and more about the pressure he put on himself. As a child, Ernie's father put tremendous pressure on him. Since Ernie was always a great player, his dad tried to take some of the credit for Ernie's success. His dad used to go to all Ernie's games and constantly told Ernie he would be a superstar in professional baseball. Ernie said that when he was a freshman in high school, he was shocked some of the older kids on the team were better than he was. Ernie had always been the best player on every team he had ever played on. His high school had a great team; many of the older players his freshman year went on to play college or professional baseball. Ernie said because his dad always told him how great he was, he was not prepared to play with players better than he was. During his freshman year Ernie told his dad not to come to any of his games, to quit talking about baseball with him, and to quit trying to live his life through his son.

Because of his dad's constant pressure, Ernie developed his own internal critical voice. Even though he hit .539 in the semi-pro league, Ernie did not have the same confidence he had while he was playing in high school. Ernie knew he put too much pressure on himself, but did not know how to change. In the semi-pro league, while at bat, Ernie would often think, "I need to get a hit." I told Ernie he was focusing on the end result he wanted to have happen, not how he wanted the result to happen. I wanted Ernie to break the process of getting a hit down much more than "I need to get a hit." I asked, "What do you need to do to get a hit?" Ernie told me, "I need to see the ball and know what type of pitch is coming." When I took it a step further and asked, "How does one see the ball and determine the type of pitch?" Ernie told me he had to be relaxed in order to see the pitch. Thus we shifted his focus from getting a hit to relaxing and seeing the ball. Getting a hit was focusing on the desired outcome. I wanted to focus on the process of how to get a hit. Most athletes spend too much time focusing on the desired outcome, not the process required to get the outcome. Focusing on the process is much more important than focusing on the outcome.

I pointed out the amount of pressure Ernie put on himself in all situations. While batting, he saw each at-bat as critical. When talking with a girl he felt that if he said one wrong thing, he would ruin the conversation. Ernie said he felt like every moment of his life was very critical and would be judged by others. Ernie was his own worst critic.

Ernie put so much pressure on himself, that when he did get a hit in the semi-pro league, it was not good enough in his mind. If he hit a single, he felt like he should have hit a double, a double should have been a triple, and a triple should have been a home run. He was never satisfied. Because he was so hard on himself, his confidence never grew or developed. In his mind, his past success was all tied to Sarah and high school. I knew we just needed to adjust his view of his experiences for him to have some success.

> Focusing on the process is much more important than focusing on the outcome.

I went to Louisiana State University, LSU. LSU has been very successful in college baseball; in the 1990s, LSU won four NCAA championships. Whenever I heard any of the LSU players interviewed, I noticed they often said the same thing: "I want to get three hits for every ten at-bats." Skip Bertman, then the baseball coach at LSU, stressed the philosophy of looking at at-bats in groups of ten. If a player got three hits for every ten at-bats, he would bat .300. Typically, it takes a player about three games to get ten at-bats, as walks do not count as an at-bat. When I explained the LSU philosophy to Ernie, he smiled a knowing smile. Instantly, he seemed to realize that if he thought of his at-bats in groups of ten, he would put less pressure on himself each time at the plate. Ernie said, "You know, instead of three for ten, I could go four for ten." While I knew this was true, I wanted to make sure Ernie did not expect to go ten for ten, as he expected in the past. He also smiled and said "If I could go three for ten with women, that would be good too."

I like to look at an athlete's best performances. I wanted to find out exactly what was working for Ernie when he was successful in high school. When Ernie talked about his success in high school, he told me while batting he simply thought, "Hit the ball hard." I pointed out the confidence in the statement, "Hit the ball hard." When he said this statement there was a firm belief that he could get a hit. His most recent approach, "I need to get a hit," was a much more desperate approach. We talked about trying to recapture the self-confidence he had in high school. As Ernie was getting ready to leave my office, he said, "Confidence is the number one reason I came to therapy." I knew I needed to address his self-confidence in each of our sessions.

Often, to get a better picture of how athletes are functioning, I look at their life outside of sports. Rarely does someone have a problem in only one area of his or her life. To get a better view of Ernie's self-confidence, I wanted to look at his self-confidence in the classroom too. Ernie said that during group discussions with other classmates in English class he was afraid to say anything. He said that in a group discussion, he would speak about 10% as much as the other students would speak. In other words, if one student talked for ten minutes, Ernie might talk for one minute. Ernie felt like he should know as much as the author of the book they were discussing. His pressure on himself to be perfect came out in all areas of his life, including the classroom. Also, Ernie said that as a kid he had a speech impediment—a lisp. Although he has worked with a speech therapist and had not had a lisp since grade school, he was still very self-conscious about speaking in public.

Ernie told me that he had a group class presentation due the next week. He was terrified and was already obsessing about speaking in front of the class. He feared his lisp might somehow come out, or that he would say the wrong thing. Many people with social phobia avoid classes where they are required to do class presentations. Knowing that I needed to deal with Ernie's anxiety in all aspects of his life, we went over the group presentation in detail.

Ernie would only need to talk for about two minutes for the group presentation, yet he was still terrified. What came out as we talked about the presentation were the unrealistic expectations that Ernie had for himself. He knew that when anyone else in the class did a group presentation, he and the rest of the students in the class forgot the presentation soon after the student sat back down. Yet Ernie felt like his presentation would be examined, judged, and ridiculed. Ernie had these same expectations when batting. If a teammate struck out, Ernie did not think twice about it. He often told the teammate, "Don't worry, you'll get a hit next time." If Ernie struck out, he felt like everyone on the team questioned his ability to hit. The fact that he was hitting over .500 gave him no confidence at all.

I suggested to Ernie that he fake his way through the presentation. I was confident that Ernie knew the material and could make a good presentation. His fear and anxiety were the only things that could foul up his presentation.

Ernie came in the following week a couple hours after his presentation and reported that the presentation went great. He said, "You know, this faking it till you make it stuff really seems to work. I was pretending to be confident—and I was." Ernie was now starting to get excited about the possibility of playing baseball again.

As Ernie progressed from crutches to the walking boot and then to a cane, we had time to really examine his fears, anxiety, unrealistic expectations, self-imposed pressure, and impatience with himself. As we dealt with each of these issues, Ernie's self-confidence began to improve. Ernie realized the need to take his rehab process in a slow and deliberate way. All throughout the Fall semester we talked about the fact that Ernie had until late January to be ready to play baseball. If he was not ready to play this season, he could wait until next season. Waiting another year was not something Ernie wanted to deal with. As he began to take a long-term approach to his whole baseball career, he became more realistic about his rehab process.

Ernie was doing physical therapy three times per week. I had to make sure Ernie was not doing too much rehab too soon. He went by the Cal coaches' office a couple times but the coaches were not in the office when Ernie stopped by. Ernie never contacted the assistant coach whom John Hughes suggested he contact. He could have called the coach and set up an appointment to meet with him, but this seemed too overwhelming for Ernie to do.

Ernie began to go to the local community college and watch the baseball team during their pre-season practice. He talked with the coaches and they were very excited about the possibility of Ernie playing for their team. The coaches told Ernie to take his time with rehab; he would be the best player on their team and they would work around his schedule. He liked the way these coaches talked to him and he quit trying to contact the Cal coaches.

As Ernie's rehabilitation progressed, I was constantly checking to ensure he was taking things slowly. Each week I checked with Ernie to make certain he was following the advice of the physical therapist and the doctor. His ankle seemed to be healing well. The doctor told Ernie that everything looked fine and that he should recover completely. Ernie began to jog lightly and started to play catch with his younger brother, now a high school baseball player. Ernie was also spending time in the weight room and was getting stronger.

I wanted to keep the focus of the therapy on the deeper issues. We began to focus on Ernie's fear and hesitation. Now that he was functioning on such a high intellectual level, he often thought too much before he acted. Hesitation does not work when trying to hit a ninety-mile-per-hour fastball. I suggested that Ernie try to be more in the moment. In other words, I wanted him to experience things while they were happening, instead of analyzing a situation after the fact. I had Ernie focus on the exercises he was doing in rehab. I wanted him to focus on each exercise as he was doing it. Often Ernie's mind wandered; he would do his rehab exercises and think about playing baseball again. He would focus on getting through a rehab session, rather than trying to get the most out of each exercise. In the past, his impatience in the rehab process led to re-injury. By focusing specifically on the exercise as he was doing it, we could make the rehab process more productive.

I also wanted Ernie to be more in the moment while batting. In the past, Ernie was often frozen by his own fear. The previous summer, while playing in the semi-pro league, Ernie seemed paralyzed by fear at times while batting. He would over-analyze what type of pitch he expected the pitcher to throw. His best hitting had been when he recognized the pitch, and then reacted by swinging. Ernie usually played second or third base or shortstop. While playing in the field, Ernie's best performances were when he did not think, but simply acted or reacted to the play. If he was playing third base and thought, "I hope I don't make an error," he often would make an error. Ernie needed to turn his mind off while playing. His head needed to get out of the way of his body. I knew if he could play more in the moment, he could continue to improve.

Ernie's fear and hesitation affected him socially too. An example was Ernie's hesitation with women. Ernie was early for class one day, and so was an attractive girl. Ernie had noticed her in class before, but had been too scared to approach her. Now, they were the only two people sitting in the hallway, waiting for the class before theirs to be dismissed. Ernie wanted to talk with the girl, but hesitated. He said she looked up from the paper she was reading and smiled at him about three or four times. Ernie was frozen with fear. He feared saying the wrong thing, or something stupid. For the next week Ernie thought of things he could have said to that girl. I wanted Ernie to be aware when he was freezing up, and then do something to take himself out of it. We talked about taking a deep breath while he was playing in the field. When batting we talked about stepping out of the batter's box, re-focusing, and then stepping back in the batter's box. With women, we talked about a couple of simple things he could say, like, "Have you started your paper for this class yet?" Ernie agreed to give these suggestions a try.

A couple weeks later an interesting thing happened one evening when Ernie was leaving the campus library. Ernie was checking out a book; as the girl working at the library handed him his book, she smiled and said, "I think you're cute." Terrified, Ernie did not say a word, picked up his book, and immediately left the library. After he had driven about fifteen minutes on the way home, he turned the car around, drove back to the library, checked out another book, and asked, "Were you the girl working here a little while ago?" When the girl said "Yes," Ernie and the girl exchanged phone numbers. Even though it is an everyday occurrence for two college students to exchange phone numbers, this was a very big deal for Ernie. Ernie had cut his lag time from days to minutes.

In our next session, Ernie reported that he was healing from the surgery quite well. Both his knee and ankle felt fine. Ernie said this was the first time since high school he was injury free. He was starting to get excited about the possibility of playing baseball again.

Ernie also reported that his self-confidence was improving too. He was talking more in the group discussions in his classes. Also, he was beginning to talk more socially. As Thanksgiving approached, Ernie knew he might have a chance to see Sarah again. Since high school, many of his former classmates met at a bar the night after Thanksgiving. Most kids were back in town to visit their families and this gave them an opportunity to get together.

In the weeks prior to Thanksgiving we talked more about his relationship with Sarah. Ernie began to realize that he did not miss Sarah as much as he missed having *someone*. He realized that he had been idealizing their previous relationship, and their time together was not as great as he liked to believe. When any relationship ends, it is traumatic. It is even often hard for people to leave abusive relationships. The beginning of any relationship is good; the end is not. Many people idealize their past relation-ships, only remembering the beginning. In one of my college classes I lecture about domestic violence. I explain that even in violent relationships breaking up is a difficult process for some people. One day after class was over, a female student waited to speak with me. She was an older student and sat in the front row each class. She always wore long-sleeved shirts. When everyone was gone, she lifted up her sleeve and showed me her upper arm. She had no tricep, only a scar where her tricep should have been. She said, "This is where my husband shot me with a rifle." Then she said, "You know the crazy thing is, I stayed with him for a year after he shot me." I knew Ernie was lonely and des-perately wanted a relationship, but since high school he lacked the social skills required to get a girlfriend. However, his social skills and self-confidence were rapidly improving.

We talked about the possibility of seeing Sarah again. Many people think therapy is about giving advice. Although I give advice at times, I believe it is better for clients to come up with the answers for themselves. I could have told Ernie, "Don't go see Sarah; it's not a good idea." Instead, I got him to talk about what happened the past four years when he saw Sarah on Thanksgiving weekend. Every year he tried to win her back, and each time Sarah rejected him again. Seeing her actually made him feel worse about himself. After we talked about seeing Sarah the past few years, I asked Ernie if he felt he would be better off skipping the get-together. He thought for a little while and said, "I think it would be better if I don't go. I don't need to put myself in a situation where I will feel bad about myself again."

As we continued to meet, Ernie's social skills kept improving. He was making much progress in dealing with his social phobia. We met the week after Thanksgiving and Ernie reported to me what had happened. He did not go to meet up with everyone Friday night and was very proud of himself that he did not go. However, the night before Thanksgiving, Wednesday, he was out with some friends. Ernie was talking with a very attractive girl and she seemed very interested in him. One thing led to another and she ended up spending the night with him. This was a boost to Ernie's self-confidence. Then the Saturday after Thanksgiving, one of his former high school teammates called Ernie and invited him to a party. The former teammate was now a well-known major league baseball player. He called Ernie and said, "Hey, I missed seeing you last night, why don't you come over tonight?" Ernie did not think Sarah would be at the party.

While Ernie was at the party, he was upstairs with some of his former high school friends. Jenny, one of the most attractive and popular girls from high school, was in the room with Ernie. They were sitting on the bed and Jenny was "hanging all over me," Ernie said. Ernie happened to look up and saw Sarah looking at him and Jenny from the hallway. They both said "Hi" and Ernie did not see Sarah the rest of the night. Since Ernie's self-confidence was improving, he did not feel he desperately needed to try to win Sarah back.

By this stage of the story about Ernie, the reader can guess he must be a fairly attractive guy. Although many women express interest in Ernie, he does not feel he is attractive at all. Ernie is bi-racial. Being bi-racial is very confusing for Ernie. Although women find him attractive, Ernie feels that he is not a good-looking guy. I wanted Ernie to be more accepting of himself, including his looks.

As Ernie continued to take his rehab process slowly, he was actually healing at a quicker pace than even he had hoped for. He started to practice with his new team. Many of the guys on the team had heard of Ernie; a couple of the kids on the team had been freshmen in high school when Ernie was a senior. Ernie was starting to take some batting practice and slowly jogging around the bases. He now realized how important it was not to test his ankle. During the rehab process, many athletes will push themselves until they feel pain. By pushing themselves to the point of pain, they slow down the rehab process and risk re-injury.

Ernie began to talk about seeing different pitches. A batter has less than a second to recognize the type of pitch approaching and to decide whether to swing or not. Ernie said he was having trouble recognizing curveballs and sliders. Here is an example where some people wonder about how much they, as counselors, need to know about the sport the athlete they are working with is playing. I only played Little League and got one hit. Fortunately, my older brother was the first base coach and told me, "Don't step off the base, the first baseman still has the ball." Had it not been for my brother, I would have been out with the hidden ball trick. It is not important for me to know what Ernie needs to do so that he can see the pitches better. What is important is for him to know what he should do to see the pitches better. When I asked, "What options do you have to improve seeing the pitches?" He thought for a minute, then told me, "I could stand in the batter's box while pitchers are throwing between starts. It would give me practice recognizing the pitches; also it would help the pitchers having a batter standing in the batter's box while they are throwing." Ernie explained to me he would not swing at the pitches, but simply stand in the batter's box with a bat, and practice seeing the pitch. Ernie's younger brother was a high school pitcher. Ernie told me he could also have his younger brother practice throwing sliders and curveballs to him.

Ernie soon played in his first practice game. This was Ernie's first opportunity to face live pitching since the summer. Ernie just hit; someone else ran the bases for him. Ernie got one hit in three at-bats. Ernie did not get a hit in his first two times at the plate. Ernie struck out in his second at-bat. When he got back in the dugout, one of the coaches praised Ernie for his hand speed. Hand speed is determined by how fast a batter can swing the bat at the ball. Fast hand speed is very important in hitters. After the coach commented to Ernie about his hand speed, Ernie realized in his first two at-bats, he was trying to show off. He felt like he needed to try to hit a home run to show everyone how good a hitter he was. Ernie is not a home run hitter. Although he can hit home runs, Ernie is more of a

> It is not important for me to know what Ernie needs to do so that he can see the pitches better. What is important is for him to know what he should do to see the pitches better.

high percentage hitter. Before his third at-bat, Ernie realized he had been putting too much pressure on himself. He refocused and said to himself, "Hit the ball hard." He quit worrying about what everyone else was thinking about him, focused on what he needed to do, then hit a double.

As the end of January approached, Ernie was almost fully healed. Ernie said his ankle was "at about 85%." Ernie felt excited and ready for the upcoming season. He was still doing his rehab exercises and making friends with his new teammates. Ernie threw a party about a week before the season started and told me, "At the party, I got phone numbers from six girls." Ernie's self-confidence had improved. His social phobia was gone.

However, right before the first game of the season, Ernie's anxiety came rushing back. Nervously, he said to me, "I created a myth in high school and I don't know if I can live up to that myth." Ernie's family, teammates, and coaches were anxiously awaiting his return to baseball. In the week prior to the first game, Ernie was not connecting with the ball. He realized he was again taking a longer swing. He recognized that during each at-bat he tried to hit a home run. Ernie began to question if he should have even tried to make a comeback. He told me, "I wonder if I even have the mental capabilities to play baseball." My reply was, "Yes, you do. I should know, I'm the expert." When I was coaching, probably the most important thing I did as a coach was to get athletes to believe in themselves. I was confident that Ernie could play good baseball if he would just relax and play. I wanted him to know I had confidence in him. It is important to note that by the time I made this statement we had been working together every week for the past six months. I would not make such a bold statement if I did not have a solid relationship with an athlete. Such a statement without a relationship is meaningless, even destructive.

I also pointed out to Ernie that in many ways he was a much

more mature baseball player. I told Ernie that he had much more experience than a kid who was fresh out of high school. Obviously, he was much smarter now than he was when he played high school baseball. Physically, Ernie was much stronger too. I was confident that every aspect of Ernie's game was better now than when he was in high school. We continued to focus on Ernie being in the moment. Ernie now had the mental tools to handle whatever came up during the baseball season.

Ernie and I did not meet again until after the season was over. Besides playing baseball, he was taking a full course load at two colleges as well as having trouble with his car. Our next session was a couple days after the season ended.

When Ernie came in to see me, he had mixed emotions about the season. He told me that the season started off pretty well—Ernie was hitting almost .500. He was one of the top community college players in the state rankings. During one stretch of games Ernie went an incredible twenty hits in twenty-five at-bats, an .800 batting average. Some of the pitchers he was facing were throwing fastballs up to ninety-three miles per hour. Ernie then slightly re-injured his ankle. Having a hurt ankle affected his batting stance. Ernie said, "I went in a slump for four games." Ernie did not get a single hit in those four games; his batting average suffered accordingly. After this four-game, two-week period, Ernie began hitting again. Then with three weeks left in the season, a base runner stepped on Ernie's ankle. Ernie finished the season with a batting average of .360. Ernie's team was one of the worst teams in the league, winning only nine of thirty-six games. Since Ernie's team was so bad, it would have been easy for the opposing pitchers to pitch around him. Often, pitchers will make an effort to not give a good hitter anything to hit. With no other good hitters on Ernie's team, his statistics are more impressive.

Ernie was still so hard on himself that he did not see the

season as a success. I told him that it was clear to me that his batting average was directly correlated to the health of his ankle. As obvious as this was to me, it was not obvious to Ernie until I said it. By the end of our session, Ernie had re-evaluated his season and felt much better about his performance.

Ernie was asked to go to Europe to play in the Italian Baseball League. The Italian League is for players trying to make the major leagues or their country's national or Olympic team. Many former major league players play in the Italian league, making an effort to get back to the big leagues. Also, some current major league players play in the Italian league in an effort to get more experience before the next season starts.

Ernie was asked to play in a local semi-pro game the following weekend. Once again, I stressed patience. Ernie needed to make sure his ankle was healed before he played in Italy. He needed to allow his ankle to recover and fully heal from the previous season. Playing in a game or two before he left for Italy could only aggravate his ankle. I wanted Ernie to still focus on the big picture of his whole career. Ernie was able to mentally step back and evaluate the situation. He had a month before he would actually be playing in Italy. He realized he would be better off using the month off to allow his ankle to heal and recover.

Ernie is a work in progress at the time of this writing. I know he has made tremendous improvement in many aspects of his life. How far will Ernie go in baseball? Only the future can tell. Regardless of Ernie's future success in baseball, I am confident he can make his best attempt to try to fulfill his baseball dreams. From our work together, I know that in ten or twenty years, Ernie will not be someone who looks back on his career and wonders "what if?" Regardless of any future success in baseball, I am confident Ernie has made personal changes that will help him in all aspects of his life.

CHAPTER 3

Greg—High School Lacrosse

Greg came to see me toward the end of his junior year in high school; he was a lacrosse player and on the cross-country team. Greg was an interesting referral. He is the son of a friend of mine, and his dad wanted Greg to work with me. From the beginning I set up clear rules with his dad and told him that he and I were not going to talk about his son's issues unless both Greg and I felt it was important to include his dad. I had never met Greg, just heard some stories about him from his dad, so I had mixed emotions about agreeing to see him. There are not many people that do the work I do, so this limits any referrals I might have made.

Greg came in and seemed a very pleasant person. Instantly, I could tell his anxiety was an issue. He was very talkative and seemed uptight and anxious. He was confused and frustrated with the level of his lacrosse play lately. At the time, I knew very little about lacrosse, but I was confident that I could help him improve his game. I do not think it is necessary for someone working with an athlete to know all the ins and outs of his or her particular sport. I knew Greg could teach me anything I needed to know.

His background, in brief, was that as a freshman he was moved up to the varsity lacrosse team. This was very unusual; he was the only freshman or sophomore on the varsity team. Lacrosse was a big sport at his school. They had a freshman, junior varsity, and varsity team. He told me that he has the best stick handling skills of any player on the team. He said that his coach, teammates, and his dad all thought he was not playing up to his ability. Recently, he was playing in a scrimmage and he missed four shots in a row—and there was no goalie. The coach had the goalies working elsewhere during the practice; Greg had four easy shots and could not make any of them.

Greg told me "I don't like to get hit." What I soon found out about lacrosse is there is a lot of hitting. The boys wear football shoulder pads and helmets; if you stand around and hold the ball, you get smashed. Greg said that when he was passed the ball and had an open shot—he froze. He described this as "dancing around." He would either hesitate and the goalie would adjust and block his shot, or more often than not, he would wait so long, someone on the other team would plow into him, and run him over. Greg spent a lot of time on the ground.

I do not think it is necessary for someone working with an athlete to know all the ins and outs of his or her particular sport. I knew Greg could teach me anything I needed to know.

When I asked Greg to explain the feeling he has when he froze up, his reply was "I remember being three years old, spilling milk and being paralyzed with the fear I would be hit." Also he said as a little kid he remembers his parents yelling at the top of the stairs while he was at the bottom of the stairs. He was terrified and frozen with the fear that his dad would push his mom down the stairs. He said that he had the same feeling when he had the ball around the crease, the area close to the goal from where many goals are scored.

The first thing I told Greg was that we did not need to address his level of play as much as we needed to get him to relax. I knew it would be a long process to implement any changes, but the first thing I wanted him to do was to be aware of his anxiety. I wanted him to notice in games when his anxiety was high and when it was at the appropriate level.

During our second session Greg told me, "I'm too nice, and that gets me in trouble." He explained that when he has the opportunity to score, one of the many thoughts that run through is head is "pass the ball and let someone else score." The problem was that his role on the team was to be a scorer. He was often passing the ball because he felt he would freeze up if he held onto it. Scoring did not seem a viable option to him.

Another fear he talked about was going for the loose ball. Lacrosse is played with a solid rubber ball about the size of a baseball; if someone misses a pass the ball often goes bouncing and rolling for a while. This creates a great opportunity for a fast player with good stick skills to get the ball on the run. Greg told me that he was scared when there was a loose ball, saying "I know I am faster and could get to the ball first, but I don't even try."

Even though we only had two sessions, I was impressed at Greg's insight, as he was aware of and able to articulate his fears. Many athletes have a hard time doing this. They often try to deny or avoid their fears. I knew that by talking about and dealing with Greg's fears, he would improve—and soon.

By our next session Greg had played two games. Even though he did not score, he was shooting more. He had nowhere to go but up in the number of shots taken. Also, he began to talk about pressure. As he described it, he often went into a downward spiral. The more pressure he felt both from others and himself, the more he would hold back and freeze up. We talked about how he was always willing to put himself last in order to help others.

In coaching, Greg would be described as a guy who thinks too much. Over the years there have been many athletes who were successful because they were too dumb to know better. What I mean by too dumb is these athletes did not think at all—they went out and performed; they did not seem to have the capacity for extraordinary complex abstract thought. Of course this is not completely true, but some athletes are not savvy enough to get scared or think about things using insight as much as Greg did.

Greg told me about his experience taking the SAT college entrance exam. He was sitting close to someone he knew was very smart. This person zipped through his test and was done well before Greg. This made Greg very nervous; he felt like he must be doing something wrong so he tried to emulate that guy on the rest of the test and did not score as high as he expected. I had him make the connection between the exam experience and a lacrosse game. He was able to see that if anyone else scores, from either team, he then thinks "Why aren't I scoring; is there something wrong with me?"

I began to address Greg's confidence, or lack thereof, and I asked him to imagine that he had confidence. I told him to describe to me how he would look and feel if he had confidence. He told me he would look smooth, and he would feel calm. I wanted him to have a vision of what we were working toward. It was at this point that he made an interesting connection. He told me his lack of confidence stemmed from his parents' divorce. He told me he thought their divorce was his fault. They were divorced when he was about five years old and I asked him if he still felt like the divorce was his fault. His reply was "yes." An interesting aside here is that I remember asking Greg's dad once when he knew his marriage was not right. His response was "at the altar." He told me he knew the marriage would not last while it was taking place. I knew that developmentally many young children whose parents get divorced blame themselves. This is why so often the advice from everyone is to tell the kids "it's not their fault." I feel there is much wisdom in this statement.

By our fifth session, I was noticing a pattern. Greg was often late to our appointments. This can mean many things in therapy. Sometimes being late is the client's way of expressing that he or she really does not want to be in therapy. Both of us had busy schedules, so we were meeting on the weekend. Typically, when clients are not at my office ten minutes after the scheduled appointment time, I call to find out why they are running late. When I called him the day of our fifth session, he wasn't home and his mom had to page him (pre–cell phone era). He finally showed up a half-hour late, telling me he forgot about our session. During the session I connected his forgetfulness to his behavior in general. On or off the field he could not make a decision. He tried to please everyone, yet he did not "take the ball and run with it." He constantly expected others to do things for him—like having his mom remind him of his appointments. I suggested he take responsibility for being on time to our sessions and I told him that we would no longer meet on weekends.

Since he came to see me toward the end of the season, we did not have the time to implement any major changes in his thoughts or behavior while playing. When I see athletes at the end of their season, I don't try to make major changes in how they perform because there is a transition time to implement any changes. During our next session, he told me he was still very hyper and did not play very well in the last game of the season. He had a very hard time asserting himself, as usual. He said since his parents' divorce he had always thought of himself last. I decided to tell him that his dad told me he knew the marriage was wrong the day they were married. Greg was quite surprised to hear this.

Fortunately Greg wanted to continue to meet with me. The

off-season is a very good time to work with athletes to make serious progress. Greg did not have the pressure of competition. He could relax, and this would give us an opportunity to get some real work done. The topic that came up next was his alcohol consumption. When he was a freshman playing on the varsity, the older players thought it was funny to "get the freshman drunk." Greg explained to me that now he drinks to get drunk, though he does not even really like the taste of alcohol, just the effect. He said he had two blackouts, chemically induced memory losses. I explained my concerns about his drinking—that he was trying to escape his problems and he was only creating more in the process. He said he only gets drunk two times a month. He said he heard and understood my concerns and said he would try to cut back on his drinking.

As our sessions progressed Greg realized that the reason he liked to get drunk was because this was the only time he felt at peace with himself. I explained that he seemed to be trying to get a peaceful and relaxed feeling by drinking and that if he could feel calm and relaxed on his own he would not need to get drunk to get that feeling. He said, "I would play much better lacrosse too."

In our sessions it became clear that Greg was never satisfied with anything. He was very hard on himself. He said, "I look out and want something and as soon as I get it I put it behind me and want more." He was able to make the connection to his experience with lacrosse. On the field he was never satisfied with himself. If he scored one goal, he felt he should have scored two goals; it was a never-ending cycle. Many athletes and coaches feel this way and see it as a good trait. They always want more and want to do better. I see nothing wrong with trying to improve, but the way Greg was, he was never good enough and he never saw himself as successful. His games were a series of failures in one way or another. It is not possible to develop as a confident athlete this way.

We started to work on ways to evaluate Greg's game without including scoring. So many athletes evaluate their success or failure only by the numbers on the board. I wanted him to be able to break down his game with scoring being one component of his game—not all of his game. I felt if he could look at other aspects of his game, he could relax and as a result score even more. If we focused solely on scoring I felt we would be adding unnecessary pressure on his game. In my work with most athletes I look for ways to take pressure off of them.

Greg decided that he could work on several different things. Even though he had the best stick skills on the team, he felt that he could improve them even more. He wanted to work on his passing, especially hitting the open man, and he wanted to work on catching the ball and getting assists. Also, he felt he could improve on his off ball movement. I told him that I remember John Wooden, the famous UCLA basketball coach whose college winning streak has never been beaten, looked at how players moved when they did not have the basketball. Greg also wanted to work on his vision of the game. He wanted to see plays develop and have good vision of the whole field.

We then went over what percentage of his shots he should aim at making. Many athletes have unrealistic expectations; often they feel they should not miss at all. Greg said that if he made 40% of his shots he would be happy, and if he made between 60 and 70% of his shots, he would feel he was playing great. This realistic concept allowed Greg to miss quite a few shots.

I then came up with some scenarios. I asked him how his game would be affected if he missed two or three shots in a row. He said when he misses three shots in a row now he does not shoot for the rest of the game. Any time he misses his first few shots he is no longer an offensive threat. I tried to get him to see that if he is making 50% of his shots, it is very reasonable to expect that he may miss two in a row and those may be his first two shots. I did this because I wanted him to have realistic expectations for himself.

Often players get into a mindset after their first few shots. If they miss, they think they are off for the rest of the game. By coming up with other ways to evaluate his game, I felt we could begin to make some changes. In the past he would rush a shot or two, miss them, and he would be done mentally for the rest of the game. Paradoxically, the less Greg focused on scoring, the more he would score.

Along with ways to assess Greg's play without focusing on scoring, we kept talking about how he should play. Part of what was holding him back at the time was tied to always wanting to please others. What also goes along with this view is avoiding confrontation at all costs. At the time he had a girlfriend he wanted to break up with, and also felt he deserved a raise for the work he did for his dad. And he felt if he started shooting more it would cause confrontation with teammates.

I tried to model ways to deal with these issues. I showed him how to ask his dad for a raise. I said, "Hey dad, I've been work-ing here longer than a lot of people. Those that do the same work I do are making more and I feel I should be paid the same as them." Greg's reply was "It sounds easy when you say it."

We had now come to a time in our work where we had clearly identified the problems, their root, and the impact they had on Greg. I felt we now really needed to focus on change. We needed to try to implement new ways to deal with all these issues. Part of the change would be asking dad for a raise and dealing with the girlfriend and teammate issues.

I told Greg I would like to talk to his dad about our sessions in that I wanted to communicate a couple things to his dad. I always clear things with the client before I say anything to his or her parents. I told Greg I wanted him and his dad to talk about the divorce, spend some time hanging out together, and talk about working for his dad as well. I could have gotten Greg to do this himself and it may have had more weight. However, I wanted them to talk soon and did not want Greg to say each week that he forgot to talk to his dad. He said it was all right for me to talk with his dad, so I did.

Things started to change. Greg asked his dad for a raise and got a small one. They talked about the divorce and his dad explained that he knew long before Greg was around that the marriage was not right at all. His lacrosse game began to improve. He was able to report on his passing, catching, vision, and off ball movement. All these areas were beginning to improve.

In the summer Greg would be attending two camps. The first camp was for cross-country and the second was for lacrosse. We met again between camps and he reported that he felt like he made a breakthrough at the cross country camp. He ran consistently with runners that he was not able to run with in the past. He felt like he was not only in better physical shape, but also mentally more together. He was approaching competition in a healthier way.

After the lacrosse camp Greg reported his breakthrough continued. He said the first three days he started off slow. He began to get down on himself and was internally yelling at himself. He realized he had internalized his father's voice. He then implemented some of the positive things we had worked on and said by the end of the camp he was clearly the best player and that the other players looked up to him.

Greg soon started his senior year of high school, which was a very exciting time for him. Cross-country season began and he was pleased with his running. He also experienced a major change. Around this time he began to take charge of his life. Greg said part of coming to see me was the hope that I would provide solutions to his problems. He realized that he needed to take charge of his life and make the changes he wanted to make. He told me he broke up with his girlfriend and felt great about it. He said, "I'm not that little kid at the bottom of the stairs anymore."

As his confidence began to grow, his attitude improved. In his previous cross-country races he would just try to stay with the faster runners. He told me that in his most recent race he and a guy from another school were going back and forth. Greg would be ahead for a while, then the other kid would pass him and lead for a while. The other kid was bothering Greg and he knew he could beat this guy. Instead of waiting until the very end of the race, Greg decided to take charge of the race. The other kid passed him one more time. Greg then really picked it up, passed the kid, looked at him and said, "You're nothing to me." Greg then took off and dominated the rest of the race.

During this time he was also practicing lacrosse and was playing much better. He worked with the goalie on his team and pointed out the goalie's weaknesses. The goalie was a bit defensive, especially when Greg said "The way you play now, I can score on you at will." The goalie did not believe him. Greg proceeded to demonstrate how he could score on the goalie. Before the shot he would announce, "This one is coming low." He then showed the goalie how to better defend the goal.

Greg was also dating someone new, who he said was always clinging to him. He did not feel the same toward her as she felt toward him. In the past he would have just stayed with her, as most prior girlfriends chose him; he did not choose them. He told this girl that he did not see their relationship progressing and they should just be friends. Now, this seems like a simple thing and it happens daily in many relationships. However, this was the first time he was able to state clearly what he wanted. Greg was now taking charge of all aspects of his life.

Greg did have some ups and downs during this time, but

the down time was less severe and short-lived. His girlfriend from last year was visiting from college. At a party she was flirting with other guys in front of Greg. This upset him and he was not sure what to do. He realized he was not happy in the relationship while they were together. She had continued to call him occasionally, even though he was standoffish. Greg decided to call her. He wished her well in college, but said he thought it was best for both of them if she didn't call anymore.

Greg's parents would often argue about finances for college. They would argue about who would pay for what expenses. Greg was able to step back from this situation and let his parents work it out, rather than getting caught in the middle, as often happened in the past.

With Greg's senior year lacrosse season approaching, we kept working on how to stay calm and relaxed during games. During the off-season his game improved dramatically. One skill he really practiced was his face-offs. The face-off is part of the game that is much like ice hockey. Two players are alone around a circle, the referee blows a whistle, and they try to get control of the ball. Greg had not been the number one person for face-offs in the past; this year he wanted to take that role.

As the season started Greg noticed something interesting; many of his teammates did not look to pass to him in a scoring situation. He had played with them for a couple years now and they were not used to looking to Greg to score. We talked about how Greg needed to call for the ball in a scoring situation and that he needed to make his off ball movement in a way that made him open to score. Also, he needed to play with an attitude that said, "I want to score." He began to make these changes and progress soon followed.

Early in the season Greg and his team attended a big tournament. The tournament had both high school and college teams, each playing in their own division. Greg was able to watch a former NCAA Player of the Year. He was able to see how this player was not tentative at all; he was very decisive and took control of games. This is how Greg had talked about wanting to play and it helped him to see how it should look. He began to emulate the player and try to take control of situations in both practice and games.

The coach began to notice that Greg was playing at a different level. In the first game Greg won every face-off, played great in all areas and scored a goal with less than two minutes left in the game. We had worked on Greg playing with more authority. As Greg began to play with more authority, his teammates also noticed a difference in the level of his play.

As the season progressed Greg continued to improve. Once in a while he would have setbacks, but they never lasted a whole game and he was able to recover fast. He found in games when his team was up sixteen to one that he did not want to score and looked to pass. He said he felt sorry for the opposing goalie. We tried to look at what he could work on in these situations to help improve his game. He said this would be a good time to work on his passing, as at times some of the players on his team that did not get as much playing time were in the game. He decided to help them score by trying to set them up with a good pass. This seemed to please everyone on the team.

Greg's playing was improving; our relationship was improving too. Interestingly enough my relationship with clients is something I just let happen. Many people talk about building rapport with athletes. When I see athletes, I try to get to work right away and ask, "What do we need to work on to improve your performance?" I don't spend time working on the relationship between the two of us; I just let it evolve. I feel if we can focus on the athletes' performance and improve their game, then our relationship will progress. Either way, the main thing is the athlete's performance. With this approach, I don't talk about my experiences or myself. I feel that talking about myself would divert attention from the main issue, which is focusing on the athlete's improvement. With Greg, it was different because of my relationship with his dad. While I saw Greg, I played racquetball with his dad every Saturday morning. Because of my relationship with his dad, if he wanted to, Greg could find out many things about me personally that other clients would have no way of knowing. However, we spent our sessions working on Greg's game. My background, or my relationship with his dad, was not important. Helping Greg improve his game was important.

I don't spend time working on the relationship between the two of us; I just let it evolve. I feel if we can focus on the athletes' performance and improve their game, then our relationship will progress. Either way, the main thing is the athlete's performance.

Greg then asked me if I would attend one of his games. I occasionally do this with athletes, as I feel it is a good way to gather more information. I always enjoy watching their games. In our next session he told me he saw me at the game and was glad I was there. He had five assists and one goal and told me he was playing with much more confidence and authority. This was clear to me sitting in the stands with his dad.

In our next session, I told him that he was the best athlete on the field. As a former coach, I feel quite capable of spotting talent and I think my assessment was correct. I told Greg it often takes time for athletes to believe what the coaches are telling them—that they have talent and they can play at the next level. I pointed out this is clearly what his coaches saw when they had him playing on the varsity team his freshman year.

Greg then brought in a lacrosse stick and ball to our next session and showed me some of his moves. This was interesting and educational for me and showed that he wanted to include me more in his life. This was during a time when the season was ending and perhaps this was his way to thank me for our work, which would probably be ending soon.

The season came to a close and Greg had his best season ever. He was very pleased with the progress he had made and wanted to continue to meet during the summer. He would be playing in college and wanted to continue working on improving his game. We continued to meet over the summer and ended up having phone sessions while he was away in college.

Greg made tremendous progress since we first started working together during his junior year. This changed his whole high school lacrosse experience and gave him the opportunity to play college lacrosse. I feel that without our work together, Greg very easily could have ended up a "broken egg."

CHAPTER 4

Tips for Athletes

Progress Not Perfection

Progress not perfection" is a concept we use in chemical dependency treatment and it applies to sports as well. This concept means you should look at the progress you have made rather than striving for perfection. The progress can be in small increments. Do not give up on your goals because you do not reach them as fast as you would like. We all want success—**now.** This view is not realistic because it is the progress you make that will ultimately take you to your goals.

Most of the time, as athletes get better, they are harder and harder on themselves. They are so caught up in the outcome of the performance that if things do not go as they expect them to go, they see themselves as having failed. They fail to notice any progress they have made, and this makes it harder for them to be consistent and to keep a positive attitude.

Perfection is not a practical goal in any sport, but it is helpful to always try to improve. Over the years, athletes whom I have seen who were perfectionists were incredibly hard on themselves. These athletes were their own worst critics. They could not live up to their own standards; each day they walked away and were thinking about what they did wrong. In the long run, all they focused on were their mistakes.

Think about why many people cannot lose weight. Often, it is because they want to lose twenty pounds—now! After a few weeks, when they have only lost a couple pounds, they give up on their diet. Wanting instant results is the reason health clubs are packed in January and February. Results-oriented people overlook the process of what they are doing. If they focus on the progress they are making and take their eyes off the desired result, they have a much better chance of reaching their end goal.

> The athlete who focuses only on winning is not looking hard enough at how to improve.

Athletes should realistically evaluate what their progress should be. They should know they will not reach their goals instantly and they should see the progress they are making toward their goals. If you can focus on progress, you will constantly be improving, which gives you a much greater chance of reaching your goals. Many young children try to improve one part of their game. They work on this new skill for a few days and then often give up because they did not see an instant change. The best skill these kids can learn is patience. Improving takes time.

Winning Is Not Everything

The concept of winning has gone too far in sports. If you are a professional athlete and winning is how you make your living, then yes, it is very important to win. Young athletes are not at the professional level and do not need to get caught up in winning. Athletes who think winning is everything and see getting second place as being first loser bring a disastrous approach to sports. This philosophy brings an end to many athletes' careers before they really have a chance to take off. The athlete who focuses only on winning is not looking hard enough at how to improve.

In the 1992 Olympics, Matt Biondi swam the fastest fifty-meter freestyle of his career. He set the World Record and won the Gold Medal in the fifty free at the 1988 Olympics (picture on cover). In 1992 he got second place and the Silver Medal.

We both were happy with his swim. The fact that he got second place did not matter to either of us at all. We were focused on what he could do, not the performance of others. Matt did what he needed to do—he swam his fastest time. We based his success on how he swam, not what place he got.

Many people do not see things this way; they overlook a very good performance simply because they did not win the competition. If they would have had the same or worse performance and won, they would have been very happy. Ultimately your main competition should be with yourself; you should look at how you did, not what place you got.

Keeping the focus on your performance and off winning is harder the higher you go in sports. As athletes progress in their career the focus is often only on winning. In high school sports, 99% of the teams end their season with a loss. If the team wins their league, they go to Sections; if they win Sections, they go to State. In my view each state does not have one team that is the winner and the rest losers. However, that is often how those who are competing see it.

Each year I see many high school athletes crying when their season ends in a loss. The season was going to end with a loss—you play until you lose. It is not the loss that is important; it is your reaction to the loss. The tears, hysterics, and anger are uncalled for. Yes, you will be upset you lost, especially if you think you should have won, but your sports experience should not be shattered by the last loss of the season.

In short, we need to be good at both winning and losing. In the end we need to show dignity and class in both our wins and losses. Sure, you should try to win the state championship. However, be satisfied with your best effort and see what happens.

Suspend Judgment and Observe

To get to the next level mentally in sports, you need to quit judging yourself. If you can do this, you can have a breakthrough. Too many athletes are judging themselves during their competition. In sports like golf, tennis, or soccer, where you are competing for hours, it is hard not to judge your own play. In a sport where the results are measured in seconds, it is much easier to suspend judgment. Suspending judgment means not criticizing yourself during the competition and, for that matter, during the season either.

Many athletes worry they are not improving fast enough. Their solution is to constantly check and judge their progress, which is an unhealthy approach. If you are doing what you need to do, you will get better. In the big scheme of things you will be on an upward trajectory, but you will have some setbacks. Constantly checking and judging your progress leads to anger and frustration. Get on the right track, and your efforts will pay off.

I have always had a bad back. Doing yoga probably saved me from back surgery. Yoga for me is simply like taking an advanced stretching class. I am fortunate that one of the great yoga teachers in the world has a studio a few blocks from my office. Rodney Yee is a master teacher. Much like legendary UCLA basketball coach John Wooden on the basketball court, Rodney is in a class by himself as a yoga instructor. While doing yoga, one of the things Rodney stresses is to accept where your body is today. What he means is, if you worked out hard the previous few days, or if you have not worked out in a while, your body may respond differently while doing yoga that day. Rodney focuses on not judging where your body is today, but accepting where your body is today. If you could put your palms on the floor while standing with straight legs last week, but can't this week, accept it—don't judge it. This is the difference between observation and judgment.

Often there are ballet dancers that take Rodney's classes. One of the dancers is so flexible that in my mind I refer to her

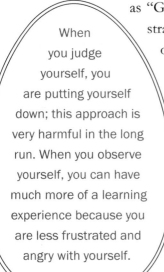

When you judge yourself, you are putting yourself down; this approach is very harmful in the long run. When you observe yourself, you can have much more of a learning experience because you are less frustrated and angry with yourself.

as "Gumby." It is incredible to see her sitting straight up on the floor with her legs straight out to each side. Then, keeping her legs straight out to the side, she can put her upper torso on the floor. The first few classes I had with Gumby, I was amazed at her flexibility. However, watching her, I had a hard time not judging myself. I would think "Wow, she is way better than me, I will never be that flexible." In order to improve my own flexibility, I had to quit comparing myself to Gumby. By accepting what my body was capable of doing, I was able to make improvements. I had to quit judging myself and focus on my body in order to increase my flexibility. If I had been judging my progress by comparing myself to Gumby, I would not have noticed the improvement I was making. The only thing I would have noticed is that I was not as good as Gumby.

Many athletes judge themselves harshly. If a golfer hits his driver great the first day of a tournament and the next day cannot hit his driver, he often judges himself. It would be better to make an observation. A judgment is, "What's wrong with **ME**, I'm not hitting my driver;" an observation would be, "My **ball** is going left today, let me figure out why." When you judge yourself, you are putting yourself down; this approach is very harmful in the long run. When you observe yourself, you can have much more of a learning experience because you are less frustrated and angry with yourself.

Suspending judgment can lead to a breakthrough. Many athletes over-think. This over-thinking often comes in the form of judging themselves. They have a critical internal voice. This internal voice is often an internalized parental voice telling them what they are doing wrong. It is time to try to put that voice to rest. By starting to observe and not judge, athletes can begin to change and start to tone down their critical internal voice.

Learn From Your Performances

Your past is your best teacher. Many athletes feel like when they compete, they are either "on" or "off," which is just not true. There are things you do that make you "on" or "off" and you need to figure them out. By looking at your past successes and failures you can start to see patterns. Ask yourself these questions: What did I do the night before my competition? What did I do during warm-up? What did I eat the twenty-four hours prior to my competition? What was I thinking and feeling before and during the competition?

One of my graduate students also coaches twelve-year-olds in soccer. After a listless performance one Saturday morning, he had each kid write down what time he went to bed the night before and what he ate before the game. Many of the kids had stayed up until almost midnight the night before the game, and most of the kids did not eat a healthy breakfast; some did not even eat breakfast at all. By learning from their poor performance, these kids were able to make changes for future games.

If you break down your performances you will see there is no such thing as a fluke. You will clearly see patterns in your performances. Most basketball players I have worked with say if they miss their first three shots in a row, they think they are off that game, so they do not shoot as much the rest of the game. If you go back to your best and worst performances, you can see what contributed to each one.

Many people can do this with their best performance, but

they do not want to look at their worst performance. However, I feel it is equally important to look at when things went wrong, because you need to be able to identify what went wrong and why. This is often when athletes see that when they were relaxed and calm things went great, but when they were really fired up they did not do as well. Most athletes need to fire down not fire up. They need to relax.

In chemical dependency treatment programs we talk about doing an autopsy on a relapse. A relapse is when someone has been off of alcohol and drugs, working a recovery program, and uses alcohol or drugs again. We have our clients go back and examine everything leading up to their relapse. Often, like athletes, our clients do not want to look at the bad in their lives. It is imperative for your learning curve to look at your bad performances. Even if it was at the end of the season, you still must examine what happened. Too many athletes figure that, "The season is over, let me put the bad performance behind me and move on to next year." This approach does not work. Next year when you are in the same situation, like the playoffs, if your memory is "Last year when I was here, I choked," you are in serious trouble. Your memory needs to be "Last year I did not do well here because...." Once you have identified what went wrong and why, you will understand why you had a bad performance and can approach similar situations with the confidence you have done what is necessary to be successful.

Do Not Tie Your Self-Worth to Your Performance

You are a person who is also an athlete; you are not only an athlete. The person who identifies him- or herself only as an athlete and lives and dies by the outcome of his or her performances is in serious trouble. Your sense of self, how you feel about yourself, should not be tied to the outcome of your performances. Once again, the higher you go in sports the harder it is to keep this in perspective. The reason it is so hard not to get tied to winning and losing is because often no one really cares about you other than how you perform as an athlete. You need to have a healthy view of yourself separate from sports. If you don't feel good about yourself, winning won't cure you.

How does one not rise and fall with success and failure? From day one, you should not get too up when you win, or too down when you lose. It is best to try to have friends that have nothing to do with your sport. The more success you have, the more you will have to work to keep a healthy balance in your life. It is often best to try to keep contact with friends who knew you before you were a successful athlete. These people may be self-conscious about keeping in contact with you because of your success, but many times they really just like you for who you are—win or lose.

> You need to have a healthy view of yourself separate from sports. If you don't feel good about yourself, winning won't cure you.

People who see themselves as athletes only are devastated when their careers end. This is because they do not know who they are separate from sports. Their whole career, their identity, was wrapped up in how they performed as an athlete. Many college and professional athletes are unable to make a transition from their sports to another career. Also, this is why some people spend the rest of their lives talking about their past successes in sports and end up trying to relive their glory days. Because their self-worth is tied only to their athletic performance, they are unable to move forward in life.

If you have interests that are not sports related, this could help you when your career is over. Try to keep up some hobby that takes you out of sports, where people do not identify with you as an athlete. If you have a large family and they don't drive you crazy, they can help you keep a healthy balance too.

Allow Yourself to Make Mistakes

In my experience, the best athletes are the ones that are able to come back from setbacks. Part of being able to come back from a setback is going easy on yourself when you make a mistake. No one is perfect; we are all going to make mistakes. I tell all basketball players I work with, "At some time in your career you will make the shot that wins the game and at some point you will miss the shot and lose the game. You need to be okay with both outcomes." Some of these mistakes are going to be big, but we have to accept that mistakes are part of sports—and life. The important thing is to try not to punish yourself for your mistakes, but to try to examine them, and then let them go. It is easier to move on when you learn from your mistakes, and once you understand why things went wrong, you will be able to move forward.

Look at your performance in terms of percentage; ask yourself what percent of your performance was good and what percent of your performance was bad. For the future, try to increase the good percentage and decrease the bad percentage. This way, you will get out of good or bad, and all or none thinking. If you played a great game and missed the shot that could have won the game—it was not a bad game—it was one bad shot. Too many people are so hard on themselves that they can not tolerate their own mistakes, which hurts their overall performances and their careers.

I get tennis players to try to lower the number of unforced errors and double faults they make in a match. Instead of looking at their play as good or bad, we carefully evaluate the number of unforced errors and double faults each match. Playing a match making zero unforced errors or double faults is unrealistic. We shift the focus from good or bad play to reducing unforced errors and double faults. Thus, their overall play improves.

Do Not Evaluate Your Performance While You Are Playing

It is often hard for athletes not to evaluate their performance while they are playing. But you should wait until after the performance, then sit down and go over how you did. If you evaluate your performance while you are playing, you can get into serious trouble. By waiting until after the performance you can avoid trying to figure if you are on or off during the game.

One basketball player I worked with was constantly critiquing herself while she was playing. If she made a mistake, she would think about it, and then make another mistake, because she was so focused on what had just happened. If she fouled someone, she would think about the foul, the referee, or her opponent. After the foul she should have been focusing on what was happening in the game as it was happening. Instead the bad call would keep her from focusing on the game for the next few minutes.

If you can wait until after the game to evaluate your performance, it allows you to focus on playing and gives you a chance to get into a rhythm during the game. Many athletes need to turn their minds off when they play. When most athletes look back on their best performances they talk about being in a zone, or say "everything just flowed." This happens because they were not evaluating how they were doing during the game; they were just doing it naturally.

Help Your Parents Help You

Your parents want to help. It is important to keep this in mind. However, you need to let your parents know if they are helping you or not. If you feel they are putting too much pressure on you, ask them not to come to your games. This sounds a little harsh, but at times it needs to happen because what they are doing to help may not be helping you at all. It is your duty to communicate with them. If they are helping or not, you should explain to them the kind of help you want.

Many times parents will feel the need to talk to their kids during halftime, or even during a game. If you do not want them to talk to you during halftime (and they shouldn't), tell them. Nine times out of ten what they want to tell you during halftime of a game, you either know, or your coach has told you the same thing. You need to let your parents know that this behavior does not help you at all.

I have seen too many kids that don't try to contain their parents; many of these young athletes end up quitting. It is not that they do not like the sport; it's that they do not like the pressure that comes with the sport. This pressure primarily comes from their parents. Let your parents know how they can help you. Say something like, "It really helps when you support and encourage me. It does not help when you try to coach me or tell me what to do." They will counter with, "I'm just trying to help." You say, "Yes, I know, but here is how I need your help…." They may not change. But if you tell them what would help you, it could be a start.

No Excuses

Do not make excuses when you are not at your best. If you lose, simply say, "good game." If you are playing poorly do not have a tantrum. Many times I see athletes who have a tantrum for the benefit of others. One basketball player thought if she put on a show, after she was called for a foul, everyone would know the foul was not her fault but was a bad call by the referee. She also would over-act when she was not making her shots, because she wanted to let everyone know she was a better player than how she was playing that day. This kind of behavior is not necessary; it usually starts a downward spiral that people cannot get out of. If you are having a tantrum, it makes it harder to turn things around and play well. You may end up playing not as poorly, but you don't end up playing great. If you are not at your best, do not think you need to explain this to everyone. Focus on what you are doing right.

Give the Referees a Break

During the course of your career you will have some calls go against you and other calls that go your way. You should not get caught up in either one of these situations. This is often a major distraction for athletes, because they allow the referee to take them out of their game. Let your coach argue with the referee. You do not need to show that the reason you fouled out was because of a bad referee. The quicker you can move forward with your game, the better you will play.

I know one high school basketball player who quickly went from averaging twelve points per game to averaging twenty points per game. When I asked him what caused the drastic change, he told me, "One game I decided not to talk to the referees at all and I scored twenty-five points; I have not talked to a referee since then." By ignoring the referees he was able to shift the focus of his game from the referees to his own play. Ignoring the referees is something I think every young athlete should try for a few games.

Good Sportsmanship

Good sportsmanship is key; we are now in the age of trash talking and showboating. Some professional athletes act this way to try to get on the highlight films. They feel showboating increases their notoriety and can help get them advertising contracts. This may or may not be true, but poor sportsmanship can take away from your performance and give your opponent an edge. Think if you are playing tennis and you see your opponent cursing and throwing his or her racquet. On some level you know you have them on the ropes. They are frustrated, openly displaying their anger, and you know you have an advantage because they are losing control of their emotions.

When your high school season finishes with a loss, go and congratulate the other team, wish them the best of luck in their next game, and do not dwell on your own loss. Good sportsmanship will help enhance your overall sport experience because you will not live and die by the outcome of a game. Also, you will develop better relationships with your teammates, coaches, and other players in the league when you show good sportsmanship. Often times you may end up playing on the same team as your opponents when you move to the next level in sports.

Keep Learning

You should be learning constantly and always have an attitude of being willing to learn. I remember watching a ten-year-old boy trying to hit a baseball before his practice started. A coach from another team was early for practice and offered a couple pointers to the young kid. The child snapped back, "I'm ten years old and have been playing baseball for four years; I know how to hit the ball." This may seem a little funny, or cute, but it is really a sad situation. Here was a ten-year-old know-it-all, who was not willing to learn; he was out of sports before high school. You should try to keep an open mind and always be learning.

Often when athletes have success, they are much harder to coach; they will go through a season thinking they know everything, only to be disappointed with the end results. Only after the profound disappointment do they ask the coach, "What went wrong?" You should constantly be learning and listening to your coaches. Chances are the further you go in sports, the more your coaches know. If you do not feel your coaches are knowledgeable then get the information you need from elsewhere, but keep an open mind. Do not be complacent in your sport. You should be constantly learning about things like nutrition, rest, weight training, and stretching. There are always new ideas. If you keep learning, it can only help you in the long run.

I also stress with my graduate students that they should always be willing to learn. Many of them have an extensive background in sports. Still I remind them of the Chinese proverb, "Wisdom begins with the words 'I don't know.'" Once you feel you know everything, your learning stops.

Some Ideas in Sports No Longer Apply

You should try to get rid of ideas that are no longer useful. In the sport of swimming, during the 1970s, there was a concept called "breaking the pain barrier." The idea was that if you pushed yourself hard enough, you would break through some invisible pain barrier inside of you. The idea was once you broke the pain barrier, you could train even harder and not feel any pain and if you pushed yourself to do this every day, you would improve a great deal.

The idea of a pain barrier was before the concept of overtraining. Overtraining is a relatively new concept in sports. In swimming this came about when some of the great coaches of the time figured out that the concept of breaking the pain barrier daily was unrealistic. They noticed their athletes were overtrained and getting worse. Thus, these coaches started to cycle their practices; one day they did sprints, the next day they did long distance. The point is that they realized the concept of a pain barrier was no longer useful and needed to be put to rest. This is one of the things that made these coaches successful—they were always looking at ways to improve.

I have already stated that the concept of getting fired up is no longer useful. The only time I see getting fired up as useful is if you are way better than your opponent is. If your team is 10-0, playing a 0-10 team, it is time to get fired up.

Instead of being fired up, athletes should have intensity and focus, yet still be calm. All three of these characteristics are important. If you have ever heard someone who runs the 100-meter dash talk, they talk about relaxing; they do not talk about getting fired up. Typically they say, "I really tried to relax the last 15–20 meters of my race." These sprinters run a 10-second event. They know that if they are too tense they will not run as fast; they have intensity, are focused, yet they are still calm and relaxed.

One professional football player I worked with thought he was a head case. His whole football career he was told he needed to get fired up for his games. He would be in his uniform, complete with pads, three hours before the game started; he thought this would help him to focus and get fired up for the game. The reason he wanted to see me was that he was having trouble in the second half of every game. He concluded that he was not fired up enough.

The more we talked, the more obvious his problem was; the second half of the game he was exhausted. He was completely and utterly drained because by the time the second half came around, he had been fired up for about five hours—this is like running a marathon. We worked to change his pre-game routine; he learned how to relax and fire down. His second-half play improved instantly because he now had much more energy during the second half.

Too often when people try to get fired up, they do not perform as well. If an athlete is a football player, his focus becomes too narrow; he does not see the whole field. This happens in many sports because being fired up does not last the whole game. Being calm, focused, and relaxed yet still intense can last the whole game.

There is a difference between intensity and getting fired up. Intensity means knowing what you need to do and where you need to focus. Simply being fired up is a waste of nervous energy. By staying calm and relaxed you do not waste your energy. Think of an animal stalking its prey. The animal is very intense, extremely focused, but calm—saving its energy to make its move. If the animal was just fired up, it would be running around all over the place with no focus at all; it may look good for a while, but in the end it would probably starve.

The more you can relax and stay calm during big competitions, the better off you will be. Just being in a big competition will fire you up. In these situations it is very important to try to fire down. You should learn how to keep your intensity up, yet still remain focused and calm. When you learn how to relax and conserve your energy, you will be able to channel your energy in the right direction—into your performance.

One other concept we need to get rid of is trying to be tough and play through pain. I have seen way too many athletes who turn a minor injury into a major injury because they would not rest and heal. Both the athlete and their coach felt the athlete should be able to tough it out. This belief has ended far too many careers, in every level of sport.

Emotional Management

You should learn how to manage your emotions. Too many people have the idea that "You have to let things go and move on." One of the things we talk about in chemical dependency treatment is learning how to manage your emotions differently. Some athletes have a hard time managing their emotions during a competition. Typically these are athletes who do sports that take some time. Sports like football, golf, tennis, volleyball, hockey, lacrosse, soccer, baseball, and basketball are dynamic and changing events. It is important for the athlete in these sports to learn how to manage his or her emotions during competition.

I remember reading a statement that said, "There is nothing wrong with having problems, the important thing is that you don't have the same problem this year that you had last year." Many athletes have the same problem throughout their whole careers. Often these are anger management problems. If athletes have problems with anger year after year, clearly they are not learning how to deal with their anger. Often athletes hope their anger will change; they may have a performance or two when they do not get angry, and then in a pressure situation, they explode. Clearly they have not learned any new skills about managing their anger.

I remember reading a statement that said, "There is nothing wrong with having problems, the important thing is that you don't have the same problem this year that you had last year."

I ask most athletes I work with, "If I was the opposing coach, how would I tell my athlete to beat you?" I also ask, "What would be the best way for me to tell my athlete to 'get in your head'?" Many athletes let their emotions get the best of them. They get frustrated and angry. One mistake turns into two or three mistakes—this turns into a bad performance. You need to learn how to keep your emotions in check. I am not saying do not get angry. What I am saying is, do not let your anger control you; you need to learn how to control your anger.

Emotional management is important in other ways too. Think about a golf tournament. Let's say you are playing with a person who is four strokes ahead of you at the start of the round. After three holes he is playing poorly and starts throwing his clubs. Even though he may still be one shot ahead of you, chances are when you see this display of anger you think, "He's losing it and will self-destruct. I just need to keep it together and I can win."

If you learn to manage your emotions, you will perform better, because you will not be reactive while playing. If you are mad at yourself, your opponent, the referee, your coach, or parents, try not to let it show. When you find yourself getting angry, try to take a few deep breaths, look around, and refocus on the task at hand. If you need to, step away, stay calm; do not let an opponent lure you into a fight. If you take the bait and lose control of your emotions, your opponent has won. They have taken your focus off your game and put it on them. With almost all the athletes I work with, I tell them that outwardly they should look the same no matter how they are playing.

A World and Olympic figure skater told me about competing against 1984 and 1988 Olympic Gold Medalist and four-time World Champion Katarina Witt. During figure skating competitions, the skaters waited in the same locker room. One by one each girl went out and performed her routine, then returned to the locker room. The girls in the locker room had no idea how the other skaters had performed unless the returning girl told others how she did or if there was some drama or hysterics. This skater told me that early in Katarina Witt's career, Katarina always returned to the locker room with the same poker face expression. Katarina looked the same after a performance if she fell three times or if she had a flawless performance. The other girls were left to guess how Katarina performed. Part of Katarina's plan in her rise to Olympic glory was to keep her emotions under control so as not to give any of her competitors an edge.

Dealing with Coaches

It is important for athletes to try to get along with their coaches. It is an unfortunate situation that many young athletes often do not get to play for good coaches. You do not have to like your coach. You have to be able to maintain a working relationship with your coach. Many adults do not really like their bosses or coworkers, yet they are able to get along with them. You should think of your coach in the same way.

There are many aspects of coaching; one is knowledge, another involves relating to people on a personal level. Many coaches need work on their interpersonal relationship skills. As a young athlete you may have a coach that you feel does not treat you fairly. You may feel he or she favors other players over you or yells at you for no reason at all. You may be correct in thinking that you are right and the coach is wrong. However, in marriage counseling we often say, "Do you want to be right, or do you want things to work out?" If you feel your coach is not being fair with you, try to work things out. Do not get caught up with the fact that you are right and the coach is wrong. You may be right, but the coach holds the power in this relationship. I have seen kids quit or get kicked off teams because they could not develop a working relationship with their coaches.

> However, in marriage counseling we often say, "Do you want to be right, or do you want things to work out?" If you feel your coach is not being fair with you, try to work things out. Do not get caught up with the fact that you are right and the coach is wrong. You may be right, but the coach holds the power in this relationship.

If you feel the coach is not being fair with you, take the time to talk with the coach after you both have calmed down. If this does not work, you may want to have your parents talk with the coach. But keep in mind the chances are you will have any coach only for a short time. You should not give the coach the power to end your sports career. Remember the longer you play sports, the more knowledgeable the coaches get. Try to get along with the coach as best you can. If you can keep your focus on trying to improve your performance, eventually you will come in contact with a good coach. And a good coach makes all the difference in the world.

Fear

First of all, you need to understand that fear is okay and you will be scared at times. But fear is an emotion you should try to manage. One of the problems athletes have is they compare their insides with others' outsides. Many times when athletes are scared and nervous they look around and think they are the only ones feeling this way. This is not true. Everyone experiences fear at some time in his or her sports career. Do not judge or condemn yourself because you are scared and nervous on the inside. Do not compare your internal feelings with others' external behavior. Simply try to relax. If you can present a calm exterior it can help you calm your internal feelings.

In chemical dependency treatment we talk about FEAR as:

F-Future
E-Expectations or Exaggerations
A-Appearing
R-Real

We try to change this to:

F-Face
E-Everything
A-And
R-Recover

Stop and think about your own fears; many of your fears are probably about the future. Are your fears based on how you think you might perform, or are your fears based on how you expect others will react to your performance? Are you scared you will not reach your goals? Do you exaggerate what you think you need to do? Many athletes think, "I have to play perfectly to win today." Do you exaggerate the strength of your opponent? When you do these things in your head, they can appear real, but they are not real.

These fears are all expectations or exaggerations about the future. Think of any situation that has caused you anxiety in the past. This could be while you were waiting in line for a roller coaster or in the waiting room at the dentist's office. Your fears in these situations were probably based on what you expected; you may have exaggerated what you thought was going to happen to you. You may have thought you were going to throw up on, or fall off, the roller coaster. You may have thought what the dentist was going to do would hurt so much you would not be able to stand the pain. In either case worrying served no purpose at all.

In general, many people's fears are irrational. Fears in sports are often not rational either. If you are playing an opponent who is much better than you, what purpose can your fear possibly serve? The energy you spend worrying about your fears is wasted energy you will not have for your performance.

How do you overcome your fears? The first thing you need to do is focus on and play your game. Do not think you have to change everything for the big competition. You should be confident in your game. Do not worry about the future. This is hard, especially late in a season when the competition gets harder. Instead of worrying about the future competition, prepare for the competition as best you can. At the start of the competition you want to feel like you have done all you possibly could do to prepare, and that you are now ready. You want to try to manage and control your fears; it may not be possible to totally get rid of your fears. However, what you can do is think of fear like a thermostat; if you turn it up too high, it gets very hot. Try to turn your fears down a little. Each time you turn your fears down, it gets easier to keep turning them down and focus on what you need to do for a great performance.

Also, do not get angry with yourself for being scared. John Hughes is a friend of mine who is a baseball scout for a Major League team. John told me that in Little League, every player is scared. The batter is scared of getting hit by a pitch, or striking out. The pitcher is scared of hitting the batter, or giving up runs and losing the game. The fielders are scared they will make an error and lose the game, or get hit and hurt by a line drive. Part of dealing with your fears is accepting them. This is why you, or your parents, should not be upset if you are scared. When you begin to gradually face your fears, your fears will dissipate. When John was coaching baseball, he would throw tennis balls to the batters. He would teach them how to move out of the way when they were about to be hit by a pitch. He also taught them how to turn and take a pitch—getting hit by a pitch in a way that does not hurt—as much. By using tennis balls, the batters' fears of getting hit slowly left because they realized they could move out of the way, or take a pitch, when they needed to. By facing their fears, they got better.

However, what you can do is think of fear like a thermostat; if you turn it up too high, it gets very hot. Try to turn your fears down a little. Each time you turn your fears down, it gets easier to keep turning them down and focus on what you need to do for a great performance.

In most big competitions everyone experiences some degree of fear. Often young athletes are scared or intimidated by their competition. The athlete who can be in the moment while he or she plays performs better. If you are future tripping, worrying about future events, it serves no purpose at all and actually drains you emotionally.

Many golfers have a hard time controlling their fears. If you are on the tee box and are afraid of hitting the ball out of bounds, how can this fear possibly help your drive? This is true even if you hit the ball out of bounds the last time you played the hole. Often these feelings of fear are followed by negative thoughts. The feeling of fear of hitting the ball out of bounds produces the thought of focusing on what you do not want to do. When this happens you are not looking at what you do want to do, which is hit a good drive.

I once worked with a college baseball pitcher, Mani, who was having trouble with his fears. Mani had been playing baseball his whole life and had been a successful pitcher. He had transferred to a new college because of his experiences with his old college coach (who was, in my opinion, incompetent). While playing at his previous college, Mani had a traumatic experience. He came out to pitch in the fifth inning. As he started pitching, he realized he had not settled into his rhythm yet, but he was confident that he could pitch well that day. However, he walked the first batter. He proceeded to walk both the second and third batters to load the bases with no outs.

Mani's coach called a timeout and started to walk out to the pitcher's mound. Mani was glad for the break and thought the coach would tell him to, "Calm down, relax and try to get the next batter to hit a ground ball so we can get a double play." Mani's coach simply walked up to him and said, "If you walk the next batter, you will never pitch at this school again." Then the coach turned around and walked right back to the dugout. Mani was shocked. He ended up walking the next batter; then the coach pulled him out of the game. Mani did not pitch again the rest of the season; then he transferred to a new school at the end of the season.

After Mani transferred schools, anytime he walked a batter he was overcome with the fear that he was going to walk four batters in a row. He thought that perhaps his new coach would say the same thing his old coach had said to him. Mani often thought about quitting baseball. He feared he could never make it as a pitcher. When he pitched, he was almost paralyzed by the fear of walking batters. I wish I could tell you things worked out great for Mani, but we only met a few times. I think the trauma from his old coach got the best of him and he ended up a "broken egg."

People who have fears like Mani often play not to lose rather than to win. This is most evident in team sports. One team gets ahead on a team they did not think they should beat. Then they get scared. This fear produces the thoughts of trying to hold on to their lead and they quit doing everything that got them ahead in the game in the first place. They watch the clock and start to play tentatively; they fear that they will blow their lead, which is exactly what happens. My belief is that often these fears are the coach's fears transmitted to the players. No matter where the fears come from, it is important to play smart, stay relaxed and focused, and put all fears on hold.

There is a difference between playing smart and playing reckless. If you play smart you may be a little more cautious, like not doing low percentage things, but you do not play tentatively. There is a fine line here, but one that is very important. You can tell the difference between smart play and scared we're gonna blow this lead play.

Coaches often say, "Talented athletes are a dime a dozen." This means that talent alone is not enough; an athlete must have more than talent to succeed. They must have things together mentally, have a good work ethic, and be comfortable being out front and winning. They must see themselves as champions and need to learn to put their fears and self-doubt aside and compete.

If you are in a situation that produces fear for you, focus on something. You could focus on your breathing, your equipment, or anything else that will keep you from looking at your Future Expectations (or Exaggerations) Appearing Real.

Comfort Zones

Too many athletes get stuck in comfort zones. A comfort zone is a level of play that an athlete feels comfortable in and seems unable to break out of. If by chance athletes happen to get out of their comfort zone they often bring themselves right back to a level where they are comfortable.

I have worked with many golfers who when playing much better than usual sabotaged their round. These golfers had made three birdies in a row early in the round and did not feel comfortable being three under par. Many times in other rounds, if they were on the tenth hole and had a horrible front nine, they could handle making three birdies in a row. It was their overall score that determined their comfort zone. Some golfers look at the leader board and are not comfortable with their names near the top. Unconsciously they move back to their own level of comfort. Unfortunately this move involves playing worse.

Comfort zones are also evident in basketball. If someone scores twenty points in the first half, he or she may not score much in the second half. I have seen many basketball players who score five points or less in the first half, then score over twenty in the second half. These players could not fathom scoring twenty points in both the first and second halves.

In swimming we used to see this all the time. Someone would get out in front, look around and see they were in first, and then slow down. They would not feel comfortable being out in front. This was especially true if they thought they couldn't beat another athlete.

For many athletes to break out of comfort zones they need to put blinders on. Blinders are used in horse racing so the horse does not look around and get distracted. The horse is unable to see anything except what is in front of them. If athletes can narrow their focus it is possible to break out of their comfort zones. I probably told every swimmer I coached to, "Swim your own race." What I meant was "Do not look around, focus on what you need to do and do it."

Another way to break out of your comfort zones is to try to do so in practice. Try to mentally put yourself in a pressure situation. If you can do this in practice it is easier to do so in games.

Stop and think about your own comfort zones. At what point would your success scare you or cause you to stop and question your play? Are your comfort zones around other competitors? Do you think, "I can't beat so and so?" To move to a new level in sports many things need to happen. One thing you need to be able to do is to try to get out of your comfort zone as often as you can. The more you get out of your comfort zone, the more likely you are to establish a new one.

Psyching Out Opponents

Psyching out opponents is trying to somehow get in their head, hoping that the opponents' performance suffers. It is an absolute waste of time and energy to try to psych out someone you are competing against. Over the years I have seen many athletes that try to do something—anything—to distract an opponent. Athletes doing these behaviors are taking the focus off themselves and putting it on someone else. There is only one sure way to psych out your opponents—beat them. Keep your focus on yourself and what you need to do, and your results will speak for themselves.

CHAPTER 5

Mike—High School Golf

Mike came to see me toward the end of his junior year of high school. He was seventeen years old and had always been one of the best golfers in the area for his age. Mike had been ranked nationally for a few years, but his national ranking had dropped from a high of 12th as a fifteen-year-old to almost 100th as a seventeen-year-old.

Mike's parents were both successful; they were actively involved in his career. His dad had been a successful golfer in his own right. Like many parents often do, he pressured Mike to go further than he did as a competitive golfer. His dad was very concerned because as he described it, Mike had been choking in tournaments lately. According to his father, Mike had been losing to players he had beaten in the past and was playing way below his potential. Mike and his dad would often argue about the specifics of Mike's golf game. Mike's mom felt she needed to step in and do something because of the increasing tension in the household. Thus, she called me.

Anyone who has been involved in sports knows that parents often think their kids should be superstars; however, Mike's coach felt the same way too. Mike's coach was frustrated with his level of play and felt caught between Mike and Mike's father. Since Mike's father was paying for the coach, he expected results.

Both of Mike's parents wanted him to get a college scholarship, and perhaps play on the PGA tour. Since Mike was about twelve years old, his parents had arranged for a swing coach to work with Mike; he had spent his summers at golf camps with famous golf coaches. When they had the time, Mike's parents would often follow him during his tournaments. They were constantly asking him "How is your game coming along?"

I spoke with Mike's mom on the phone for a while when she initially called me. She described the increasing tension in their household. She said she and her husband often argued about the best way to deal with Mike and his golf game. She said Mike's dad did not see the need to get a "shrink" involved; he felt that Mike should just get tough and play better. However, he too was concerned about the frequent arguments he and his wife were having. Mike's mom said she felt it would be best if I met with her and her husband before meeting with Mike. While on the phone with her I went over confidentiality, how I conduct my sessions, and my fees and cancellation policy. We set up a session for later in the week.

When I met with Mike's parents I could tell his dad had considerable control, anger, and entitlement issues. He did not seem like he was a good listener at all. It appeared as though he was barely paying attention to anything his wife or I had to say. He seemed to think that if Mike would just listen to him and do what he told him, then Mike would play much better. I suggested that Mike come and meet with me and if he did not feel seeing me was beneficial, he could decide to stop seeing me. I met with his parents for my usual 50-minute session. At the end of the session when I asked if they wanted to leave a check or mail one to me, his dad was shocked and indignant, saying, "You're charging us for today?" His wife instantly calmed him down and said she and I had discussed my fees on the phone. His dad seemed to feel like I should pay him for the sage advice he gave me on what Mike needs to do to in order to be a successful golfer. This incident was my first glimpse of the pressure Mike must be dealing with from his dad on a daily basis.

When I met with Mike, he seemed open to see me instantly. In our first session he told me he was having a hard time playing because of all the pressure he felt. He explained that his father was really pushing him to live out his own unfulfilled dreams as a golfer. Mike reported that when he was about twelve years old his dad told Mike that if he beat him on a round of eighteen holes before he was sixteen, he would take Mike and a friend to watch any PGA event anywhere in the country. When Mike was a sophomore he and his dad were playing a round of golf. Mike was well ahead of his dad with three holes to go. Mike reported that he could see his dad getting angrier and angrier each of the last three holes, knowing he may lose to his son. Mike ended up beating his dad over eighteen holes, but his dad did not make good on the bet. His dad said he had already spent enough money on Mike at that point in his career.

As our first session began, Mike started by explaining what had happened lately. He said that his sophomore year was a disappointment and that he wanted to regain the ranking he had at the end of his freshman year. He stated that he had often fallen apart during the last round of tournaments. He told me that at times he threw his clubs, something he was not proud of. In his last tournament, after he hit a bad approach shot to the green, Mike slammed his seven iron into the ground and bent the club. After the round was over he broke the club in half, then threw it away; he said it was unusable anyway.

Athletes often get into emotional patterns in sports. By this I mean a twelve-year-old who throws his clubs will often become a twenty-year-old who throws his clubs. This is true in every sport. How someone reacts emotionally seems to get fixed in time. They grow and develop physically, but emotionally they often act the same as they did many years ago. Mike clearly had some emotional patterns that seemed to be fixed in time; I knew we needed to address these issues for him to improve.

The other issue that came up from both Mike and his parents was his rituals. His parents were concerned that Mike was doing too many of these rituals. Mike described himself as superstitious. He said he would compulsively line things up like golf balls and tees. He would also fold his clothes and towels in a special way before a competition. Both Mike and his parents were concerned that these behaviors had gotten out of hand. It was to the point now where Mike would not want to go out on the course unless he felt like everything was in proper order.

Many athletes are superstitious. They have either their lucky way of doing something or an item they need to wear or carry. I see this as an attempt to gain control. By having a ritual athletes think the ritual will help control the outcome of the event. Although we know that these superstitions do not make sense, many athletes truly believe in them. What I set out to do with Mike was to look at what he could do in his preparation and play to control the outcome of his round. I was not concerned with what he wore or carried with him on the course. I wanted Mike to understand that a properly folded towel did not help his score and his rituals were a way for him to channel his nervousness into something else. If we dealt with the pressure he felt and his nervousness, he would overcome his rituals.

Both Mike and his coach said he over-thinks. He often does not play the hole he is on because he is constantly thinking ahead to the next shot, or the next hole. Mike seems to spend much of his time wondering what the other golfers in the tournament are doing. He also said that he always expects himself to win. I asked "Why?" His reply was "Good question." What was becoming obvious to me was that once Mike thought he could not win, his golf game fell apart.

I discovered that Mike played differently against different opponents. Some of the tournaments he played in were match play. In match play tournaments you play your opponent one on one. The overall score does not necessarily matter, if you both get a six on a hole, you tie the hole. If you get a three on a hole and your opponent gets a six you win the hole, but the overall score does not matter. The only thing that matters is who wins the most holes.

When Mike was fifteen and ranked 12th in the country, he played in a match play tournament. He beat the third ranked player the first day and the next day he lost to an unranked player. My initial response was "There is something wrong with this picture." Mike had lost to unranked or much lower ranked players in the past too.

Mike stated he was a perfectionist. Many athletes use this term, but there are pros and cons about perfectionism that need consideration. For Mike perfectionist meant that he was not allowed **ANY** mistakes in a round. Anyone who has played golf knows this is not a reasonable approach. I knew we needed to work on managing mistakes, not preventing them altogether.

With all these things coming up in the first session or two, I felt like I had to do some damage control to stop the emotional bleeding. What was happening now was that Mike would hit a bad shot, yell at himself, then he would hit another bad shot. The bad shot worked in a circular fashion. A bad shot would tell him he was choking. By yelling at himself, he would tell himself he was not good enough and of course the next mistake would soon follow. His perfectionism was really working against him.

The way I dealt with this was to have Mike reframe his experiences. When he hit a good shot, I had him say to himself, "That's like me. I am a good player. I hit good shots." When he hit a bad shot, I had him say, "That's not like me. I am a good player, but even good players hit bad shots."

This approach sounds simple, but actually takes a while to implement. I knew that reframing his internal view of himself was a way to get the good experiences to stick with him. Mike, like many athletes I have worked with, quickly forgets the good. Because he expects the good, he stays focused on the bad. If Mike was playing a great round and hit a bad shot on hole number fifteen, he would feel like he ruined the round. He was not able to look at the fourteen holes he played well; he expected perfect play the whole round. He only focused on the bad shot or dumb mistake on the fifteenth hole. When this happened he would think "Oh no, here I go again." Clearly, we needed to work to change this pattern. I knew it would take time, but I wanted Mike to start working on it now. I knew that for his career to get better, we had to change his self-talk—soon.

It was fortunate that during the summer Mike had the opportunity to play with one of the top collegiate golfers in the country. His name was Guy and he played at the same home course where Mike played. There were times when Mike and Guy would play together. He told me that on one hole Guy hit two balls out of bounds. I asked how Guy reacted. Mike said, "It didn't phase him; he may have even played better after that." I wanted Mike to play more like Guy. I told him to try to copy Guy's calm demeanor.

When I asked Mike what his coach thought of his play, he told me his coach said he should focus on his game, not his opponents. Mike's focus was way too broad. He was constantly worried about what the people he was playing against were shooting. He also would wonder what his opponents thought about him as a person. Also, he wanted to know what score was leading the tournament for the day and how far back he was from the leader. I worked to narrow his focus and tried to get him to focus on his shot and his game alone. I knew this would take time, but I wanted him to start with his game, not his opponent's game.

I stressed that if he wanted to be ranked in the top ten in the country, he should start acting like a top ten player. In recovery from chemical dependency acting "as if" is called "fake it till you make it." Mike felt like he could not act the part of a top ten player until he was ranked in the top ten. I wanted him to change how he acted to help get the ranking. I felt like he had to be able to act the part in order to achieve the ranking.

This all tied into Mike's level of confidence and his belief (or lack thereof) in himself. He felt if he had a high ranking he would be more confident. I wanted him to act and play confident. I knew that the ranking would be a byproduct of this action. Mike had it backwards: the ranking does not produce confidence, confidence produces the ranking.

In Mike's match play, he would often wait for the other player to make a mistake. He waited for the other player to give him the match. I wanted him to see that it was his role to take the victory, not passively wait for someone else to make mistakes.

This is where Mike's over-thinking was coming into play. Instead of focusing on his game, he was thinking about the other player and waiting for the win to come to him.

> This all tied into Mike's level of confidence and his belief (or lack thereof) in himself. He felt if he had a high ranking he would be more confident. I wanted him to act and play confident. I knew that the ranking would be a byproduct of this action. Mike had it backwards: the ranking does not produce confidence, confidence produces the ranking.

There was another golfer Mike played with named Keith. Keith was a year older than Mike, a senior in high school and a rival of Mike's for several years. Anytime they played together, Mike felt like he had to beat Keith. Even though this was supposed to be a practice round, there was no **practice** in the round; all Mike focused on was beating Keith. Even when they hit balls together on the practice tee, Mike focused on whether his balls were going farther than Keith's. Mike was unable to focus on trying to improve his game; he was stuck focusing on beating Keith.

I pointed out to Mike that because of all these issues he was not improving. He was trying to hold on; he was not doing the things he needed to do in order to get better. Because of pressure and distractions he was not working on the things his coach wanted him to work on to improve his game. Mike's coach wanted Mike to focus on his swing, movement of the ball, and his touch and feel for the game. By focusing so much on the outcome, Mike was completely ignoring the process. By process, I mean the gradual improvement in the areas his coach said Mike could work on improving—like putting and chipping. If he could make improvement in the above areas, Mike's game would improve in the long run.

Mike was able to notice the difference in how he played when he was playing with Guy and with Keith. When playing with Guy, Mike encouraged himself more, and tried to keep up with Guy. It seemed when playing with Guy, Mike's game rose to Guy's level. When playing with Keith, Mike was preoccupied with not losing; he would yell and berate himself if Keith was beating him.

I found this observation encouraging. At least Mike was now aware he was playing differently with each player. I had him try to approach his game and play each day like he did when he played with Guy. I also wanted Mike to notice when he was yelling at himself while playing with Keith. Awareness is often the first step in correcting any problem.

As time went on Mike started to show signs of improvement. By noticing when he was yelling at himself he was able to start to implement some changes. He would take a deep breath and then say "That's not like me, I'm a good player." At times he would alter the wording, but the internal message was still the same. He also started to notice how many good shots he actually did hit. He started to cement these experiences as material instead of glossing over them because of his unforgiving expectations.

Mike's practice rounds started to get better, but in his first tournament since we started working together Mike played about the same as he played prior to our sessions. His parents were concerned and began to ask him if working with me was helping or hurting his game. He wanted his parents to back off, but did not know how to talk to them about this. This was another example of his parents' over-involvement. True, they were concerned about what was best for him, but they did not seem to know when to give him private space.

We went over how Mike could talk to his parents. We focused on how they wanted to help. They would do anything they could to help Mike. We had to redefine help. Help was not his dad going over each shot after every round. Often, the drive from the course back to the hotel consisted of Mike's dad giving his critique of Mike's round. This review often lasted through dinner. Any time dad thought of something to add he brought it up to try to help Mike improve. Luckily, Mike's mom was on our side. She would give words of encouragement, like, "You'll do better tomorrow, don't worry about it."

Before the next tournament, I had Mike educate his dad on the help he wanted from his father. His coach would also be at the tournament. We wanted his coach to do the coaching and his dad just to be dad, not dad/coach. Mike asked his dad not to comment on his game unless Mike asked him for his opinion. After the tournament dad could give a brief synopsis of the round, but it was up to Mike to decide when his dad had said enough.

What happened over the years is that Mike internalized his dad's critical voice. From his dad constantly correcting Mike over the years and pointing out what Mike did wrong, Mike began to do this on his own. What we were really trying to do was silence the inner voice of Mike's dad in Mike's head. I think this is where Mike's perfectionism started, which led to his rituals. The rituals were done to try to calm dad's critical internalized voice.

At the next tournament, Mike played better. He was more consistent; he still made some mistakes, but came back from them quite well, placing higher than he had recently. When he got home, Mike had his best round in years while relaxing and playing eighteen holes with his friends. He was wondering why he could not play that well in a tournament. My focus was to make Mike understand that he was playing well and that it was just a matter of time until he played that well in a tournament.

As summer started, we were not going to be able to meet for five weeks. He and I were both going to be away; there was nothing we could do about it. Because he would be playing in four tournaments in those five weeks, we went over the things he should be focusing on until our next session.

During our next session, Mike quickly told me what had happened. The process by which someone changes usually has a transition period. During this time, there are highs and lows, but the lows are not as deep or as long; however they are still there. Mike reported that at one tournament in particular he had a scene. When we got to the bottom of it, we discovered he was playing badly and felt like he had to throw a fit to show everyone that he was playing badly. In other words, his scene was for them. He felt like if he acted very upset with his play, others would know he is a better player.

It was at this point that I asked Mike to sign a release of information form so I could talk with his coach. I wanted to get his coach's perspective on the whole situation. Mike's coach and I had a good conversation. His coach narrowed it down to four things that he thought Mike needed to work on. First of all, he said Mike always looked for excuses for bad play. The second thing ties into the first. He said Mike does not own his mistakes, which is where his club throwing comes into play; Mike acts like it's the club's fault for a bad shot. The third thing the coach pointed out that Mike needed to work on was his level of frustration. The fourth thing was Mike's tendency to give up when things aren't going his way.

Hearing this information from the coach was very helpful for me. These are weaknesses I tried to address and I knew these problems would take more time to change. Mike had a big tournament coming up in two weeks and he was getting impatient. I stressed patience with Mike. I knew that over time Mike would get better. His frustration with his game was evident in our work together; he wanted results from our work exactly the same way he wanted results on the course—instantly.

The big tournament would be match play. At the tournament, Mike beat the 20th seed of the tournament. He was then playing the 5th seed; they were even with four holes to go. The last time he played the 5th seed, the match was over with six holes to go; in other words Mike was down by seven holes with six holes left to play. Being even with four holes to go, Mike started to think about the outcome of the match. If he could beat the 5th seed, his ranking would move much higher, then he would play one of the top-ranked players in the next round. The more his mind began to race forward, the less he was focused on the task at hand. He lost the next three holes in a row and the match was over.

Mike was aware of what had happened. He was relying less and less on his superstitions and was depending more and more on himself. He said, "I wanted to win so bad." I felt that Mike seemed to know what he needed to do; he was just having trouble implementing the necessary changes in the heat of the match. He knew that when he started to focus on winning, he was not focused on hitting each shot.

His parents told him they were beginning to notice a difference in Mike's attitude and play. They commented to him that he was playing much better overall and he seemed to be handling stress and pressure much better. However, his dad still said that Mike had no fire in him. We had worked on managing his emotions on the course, in contrast to his dad, who wanted Mike to be emotional while playing.

Mike had a span of time where he would be in town for a week, so we met three times in six days, giving us a chance to do some intensive work. I was encouraged because I was starting to see progress in Mike. His awareness had definitely increased and he was starting to notice when things were getting out of control and was trying to implement changes. Another encouraging sign was his play in practice rounds. When Mike played with friends his overall scores were consistently getting better. I felt that it was only a matter of time before Mike started to have better rounds in tournaments.

We kept trying to focus on what Mike wanted to do in his game, rather than what he did not want to do. In his next tournament Mike finally seemed to put it all together. He made the cut and each round was a solid performance. His confidence started to grow. I could see that his attitude and belief in himself were improving.

Mike began to focus on playing one shot at a time, rather than playing the whole tournament at once. In the past, he would show up at a tournament, guess what score it would take to win or to get in the top ten, then go out and try to shoot a score that fit his predictions. In other words, he was trying to play the whole round, rather than one shot at a time. We shifted his focus to each shot. Once again, this sounds very simple, but if your last shot was a bad one and the next hole is the hardest on the course, this is very challenging.

Mike could instantly see the importance of this approach.

In the past he often got into trouble with four holes left and he would try to par out. He would be on the 15th tee and say to himself, "I need four pars here." The problem with this approach is he was not planning his 15th tee shot. Often, his attempts to par out led to him being three over par for his last four holes—or worse. Mike began to see that almost every time he began to look at what he felt he had to do on the last four holes, he made unnecessary mistakes. He also noticed that he never needed to play as well as he felt he had to, meaning if he would have relaxed and played the last four holes one or two over, he would have been fine.

As his golf game started to progress, Mike seemed to be a little distant during the beginning of our sessions. He even said, "I'm not sure I need to come here anymore." I felt this was because he felt that as long as he had to see me, he was a head case in his own eyes. Once the sessions got started he seemed to relax and realize our work together was helping him. For me, working with athletes is interesting work because, obviously, one of my goals in working with anyone is that they eventually don't need to see me anymore and capture a greater mental health and happiness. Mike commented that his coach said he was making progress and was quite pleased with his play lately. We talked about his conflict about coming to see me. Part of him did not want to see me and part of him did want to keep working with me. I told him this was okay and when we both agreed we should stop, we would stop. Mike realized that our work was not yet done and that we still needed to meet to keep his success going.

One of the ways our work shifted was that we were working on the difference between knowing Mike does not have to win and feeling like he does not have to win. Knowledge is one thing. Many people often know what they need to do; however, emotions do not always follow the mind. Mike knew he did not have to win, but he felt pressured to win. We worked on his awareness, taking a deep breath and relaxing when these feelings came up. Another way we worked to cope with his emotions was focusing on the task at hand, which would help keep those feelings of pressure under control.

This approach worked. Mike had his first top ten finish in years. He was very happy and relieved. Things were beginning to fall into place. His self-talk was changing and he was feeling more confident.

The summer was over and although Mike was making progress, I knew he could improve even more. Since he would not have any tournaments for a while, it was a good time to work on the changes he needed to make. Often, I get called when the season is almost over. Parents and coaches often focus on the big competition that is coming up, then after it is over, they don't worry until the same time the next year. I knew that with Mike we could make some real progress if we continued to meet during his down time.

We began to explore the pressures of Mike's senior year in high school. He wanted to enjoy his senior year, keep his grades up, and get a scholarship; he also wanted to enjoy golf. During the past summer he started to finally enjoy golf again. Before we started meeting, Mike played with so much fear and worry there was no enjoyment in his game at all.

Mike was still in a transition phase as far as I was concerned; he had to work on his anger, self-talk, and emotional control because it was not habit yet. One of the things we worked on was keeping an even keel with his emotions; I wanted him to look the same on the outside if he was two under par or five over par. We talked about what this would look like on the course. Luckily he played enough with Guy that he saw what emotional control should look like.

We also came up with a more detailed strategy to deal with

his father. Mike's first big tournament was over Thanksgiving and he did not want his dad to go to the tournament; Mike felt like he could play better without his dad around. He felt as though there would be less pressure on him if his dad did not go to the tournament. This was a precarious situation. Mike's dad was paying for Mike to see me. If I/we decided he should not go to the competition, he might think seeing me was not a good idea and might insist Mike not see me anymore. Dad's attitude was still, "Mike needs to be able to play under pressure." Therefore the dad's harassment/pressure justified any of his actions, because in his mind, if Mike could not deal with his dad's pressure, how could he deal with the pressures of college golf or the PGA tour? I agreed that Mike needed to be able to play well under pressure; however, we needed to remove unnecessary pressure and his dad was unnecessary pressure.

Mike's dad reluctantly agreed to stay home and for Mike to go to the tournament with his coach. With the dad issue settled, we began to look at Mike's comfort zone. Our focus in the past had been to try to get Mike to keep his emotions under control and not self-destruct. We had been trying to have Mike keep his game on course when things started to go bad. Now, I wanted to focus on how Mike would handle his emotions when playing a great round. It is one thing to try to contain your emotions when you get an eight on a hole; it is another thing to contain your emotions when you are having the best round of your life.

I asked Mike how he would feel if he made three birdies in a row and what would happen if after the first round or two he was in first place? How would he react if he was playing with and beating a higher rated player? How could he keep his emotions in check if he was putting to win the tournament? This would be an out-of-state national tournament and all of the top high school golfers would attend. Many college coaches would be at the tournament to see how the top recruits played under pressure.

Mike's national ranking climbed to 20th over the summer. He was pleased with the improvement, but wanted to move up even more. He seemed ready to make a jump. His practices were going very well, his scores were better than ever, and he was keeping his emotions under control.

In the Thanksgiving tournament everyone plays two rounds; only the top fifty players play in the last two rounds. All of our time working together we focused on what Mike needed to do to play good golf. I purposely told him there was no reason to focus on things like making the cut or winning the tournament. He needed to play good golf and let the chips fall where they may.

We spent a lot of time leading up to the tournament focusing on one shot at a time because many golfers have one bad shot and it turns into two or three bad shots; some have a bad hole and it carries over onto the next hole. We looked at how each shot could be an entity unto itself. For this to happen it would take concentration, focus, and relaxation. Mike had been working on this for months and things seemed to be coming together.

After the first two rounds of the tournament, not only did Mike make the cut—he was in the top five. He put together the best two rounds he had played in years. His parents were ecstatic; they could not contain themselves and flew down to watch the last two rounds of the tournament. They told Mike they would keep their distance, but they wanted to watch him play.

The third round Mike played even better and he was now in the top three; his game was consistent and solid. He was able to keep his emotions under control; one bad shot was just one bad shot. He had the confidence he could recover if he was in trouble and he did recover anytime he had a setback. His fourth round was just as good and Mike finished the tournament in the top three.

This, obviously, was a huge breakthrough for Mike; one of the top college coaches who had Mike on his "B" or even "C" list offered Mike a full scholarship. Mike was very happy as he explained the tournament to me. Then an interesting thing happened—Mike said he did not need to see me anymore. This has happened to me in the past; often when athletes have success they feel like they don't need to see me because deep down, on some level, they think because they are seeing me, it means they are a head case. As we often say in chemical dependency treatment, "They get well too quick."

I told Mike since he did not have any tournaments for a while, we could wait and meet after the Christmas break. Since he would be out of town over the holidays, we really were only taking a few weeks off. However, we did not meet again until February. By this time, he was starting to get ready for his high school season. He was still feeling good about his game and would only be playing in local tournaments for a while. His next national tournament was not until Spring Break—about eight weeks away.

We reviewed Mike's progress and took a look at what he did that caused the changes that improved his game. I feel this is very important. I wanted to review the changes he made, so that in the future when we were not working together, he could make any adjustments by himself. In the past, he saw much of his success as luck. I wanted him to know his success came from changes he made, so he would feel more in control of his overall game.

After a few weeks of working together again, another interesting thing happened. Both his coach and his mom called me in the same week. This was unusual, as I had only talked with his coach one time a few months ago. The coach was concerned:

"Mike was testing himself daily." He said that if everything did not feel perfect, Mike would start to get upset. With the National Tournament approaching, he said Mike was putting pressure on himself to repeat his Thanksgiving performance. His mom basically said the same thing; she saw his stress level rising and wanted me to be aware of what she was seeing. She also said that Mike's rituals, which had almost completely gone away, were now returning.

I relayed these conversations to Mike the next time I saw him, as this is a standard policy of mine. If I am working with high school athletes, at the beginning of our work together I tell them I will relate to them anything their parents tell me. I also tell them I will only give their parents information the athletes want me to give. This way our relationship is solid and they do not have to worry that I am talking behind their back with their parents or coach. When I speak with an athlete's parents, I start the next session with "Your mom called and this is what she said."

> In all my years as a coach and a therapist I have come to my own conclusion that there is no such thing as a fluke. If you did it—then YOU did it—it did not just happen. Believing a performance was a fluke comes from a lack of

Our next session I started with "Your mom AND your coach called me; here is what they said." Mike explained that he was worried the Thanksgiving tournament was a fluke. Many athletes use this term. In all my years as a coach and a therapist I have come to my own conclusion that there is no such thing as a fluke. If you did it—then **YOU** did it—it did not just happen. Believing a performance was a fluke comes from a lack of self-confidence.

Mike was now experiencing the pressure that successful

athletes experience. It was one thing for Matt Biondi to break a world record; it was another to be the guy that everyone was trying to beat for years. This is a different form of pressure and it takes its toll on many top athletes. They have focused on how to get to the top and once they are there, the pressure changes; now they are the person everyone is trying to beat. Mike's top-three finish at the Thanksgiving tournament put more pressure on him; he felt like he had to finish in the top three again.

Another interesting thing was starting to happen; I was feeling pressure too—so I set up a consultation session. Consultation is where I go, pay a therapist, and talk about the client I am seeing; it is like therapy about my therapy. I used one of my old supervisors from graduate school. I had worked closely with her in graduate school and met with her when I needed consultation on a case. During our session, she got me to see the pressure Mike must be feeling, because if I am feeling some pressure then Mike must be feeling a lot more pressure. Her advice to me was "Stay the course." She said I needed to do the same thing I was telling Mike to do—I needed to trust the process.

When Mike and I met again we talked about his need to feel great every day. We also talked about the need to prove his performance was not a fluke. I told him he needed to relax and trust himself, his game, and the process. He was able to see the pressure he was putting on himself; his reply was, "You're right, I need to pull back." Luckily, we still had a couple of sessions before he left for the tournament.

This tournament was across the country and it would take a long flight to get there. Now, I went into my coach mode a little. We always told our swimmers to bring water bottles and food on the airplane; we did not want them to get dehydrated on a long flight. Also, many athletes eat like horses; the small amount of food on a plane is not enough to satisfy a high school or college athlete. We talked about what Mike could bring with him on the plane and we went over where he would be staying, what the golf course was like, and how long he would practice before the tournament. We talked about how much time he would spend hitting balls, chipping, and putting, as well as how much free time he wanted before he teed off.

Like most athletes I work with, Mike and I went over every detail, so when he got to the tournament there would be no surprises for him. I also told Mike to prepare to feel bad when he got to his destination. This may sound strange, but when I coached this was important to do because many times when you fly across the country you don't feel right. When I coached, what we ended up doing to calm athletes was to predict for them. Telling them that they may not feel good after a long flight helped them relax when they did not feel good on arrival.

As Mike left our last session, before he left for the tournament, he stopped at the door, looked at me, and said, "Say good luck—it's good luck." I did not realize that when he left for any tournament I unconsciously said "Good luck." I did say "Good luck" to him and also said—"You don't need luck—you're ready."

Mike had a solid tournament and finished in the top five again. We only met two more times—once again he was not sure he really needed to see me anymore. Also, he was very busy with the end of his senior year; then he had summer tournaments and would be off to college. I could only hope that he could apply what we had accomplished to his future career.

CHAPTER 6

Guidelines for Parents

Progress Versus Results

Parents should look for progress rather than focus on results. They should focus on progress throughout their child's career. Young kids often see other kids who can do things better than they can. In any sport there are some kids who develop faster than others. Shorter kids are often the better athletes because the short kids are more coordinated than their taller peers are. It frequently takes tall kids time to grow into their bodies.

It is best to compare your children to themselves. By comparing kids against themselves you set them up to succeed. Most kids hit a foul ball before they get a base hit. They need to see the foul ball as a success, not a failure.

Almost instinctively, kids will look at what other kids can do, then judge themselves accordingly. You must start early and try to avoid the serious consequences of this behavior. If kids get into the habit of constantly comparing themselves to others, they will have the attitude of, "If I can't be the best, then I won't play." This attitude is a disaster. At some time when they move up, by league or age group, they will not be the best athletes—the older kids are typically better. Kids with this attitude will have a hard time playing and getting better because all they see is that other kids are better than they are.

Here are some other things that can happen if they start to compare themselves against their peers. First of all, the athlete will only be results oriented. Kids need to be process oriented. It is the process of improving, rather than the improvement itself, that is important for the long-term success of any athlete. An example is a kid in his or her first swimming competition. If the athlete simply looks at the result, did I win or beat a certain competitor, he or she misses many important concepts. The important process is the process of improving his or her personal performance. Learning the proper stroke, the way to breathe, kick, and dive, is what's important. The result is how fast the athlete swims, but the process, in the long run, will determine how fast an athlete swims. Many swimmers, like Matt Biondi, did not hit their prime until they grew into their bodies. Although Matt had some success in swimming when he was younger, in the year 1984 alone, in the 100-meter freestyle, he improved from 250th in the USA to fourth, earning a spot on the 1984 Olympic team. He was described at the Olympics as "A water polo player who came out of nowhere to earn a spot on the Olympic team." Athletes like Matt learned the process of improving long before they ever got the great results.

Anyone who coaches high school athletes will tell you they have seen kids who could have been great athletes, but these kids did not know how to train. When these kids were younger success came easy; they were always the best kids on the team. Thus they never learned the process it takes to improve. When they were younger, they just showed up and were the stars; but in high school, when everyone caught up with them, they simply quit, because they did not know or understand the process of improving.

Another thing a result-oriented athlete develops is called negative self-talk. This is the internal dialogue any person has with

It is the process of improving, rather than the improvement itself, that is important for the long-term success of any athlete.

him- or herself. In sports this negative internal dialogue is called self-talk. If young kids are constantly comparing themselves to others, chances are they end up seeing themselves as less than others. "I suck" and "Everyone is better than me, I can't get a hit" are examples of some early forms of a negative self-talk dialogue developing.

Negative self-talk has many implications. Many kids do not want to participate in sports if they are not as good as their peers. It is not important how good an athlete is at the age of eight or ten. Too many parents are worried about their young child's performance. There is very little, if any, correlation between how good an eight- or ten-year-old is, and how good of an athlete he or she will be as an adult.

Parents' attitudes and behaviors contribute to the development of the child's self-talk. If the parent is constantly critical, over time, the child internalizes the parent's critical voice. They establish the belief that they are never good enough for anyone. While many parents think it is good for their kid never to be satisfied, the harm is in the child never feeling a sense of accomplishment. Another harm in negative self-talk is that this internal voice produces doubts. These doubts come out not only in sports, but also later in life in school, work, and relationships.

When children have internalized their parents' negative voice and their own self-talk is bad, the next thing that happens is burn-out. After many years of not feeling good enough, the child's relationship with the sport changes. They may start off loving a sport but after years of not being good enough, children will question why they are participating in the sport at all. They cannot love the game if they walk away each day with a negative attitude, looking at the mistakes they made.

Lessons

One helpful thing parents can do is get lessons for their child.

The best route is to search for a qualified person to teach your child proper technique. Many college coaches spend a considerable amount of time trying to correct flaws in technique that have come from practicing the wrong technique for years. As coaches often say, "**practice does not make perfect—practice makes permanent.**" If a child keeps practicing something the wrong way, he or she will get good at doing the task the wrong way. Lessons are a way to help avoid this problem.

Lessons also help focus on the process, because anyone who teaches lessons does so in a step-by-step manner. The person teaching the lesson will focus on the steps necessary for the task to be done right. If they are teaching how to shoot a basketball, they will look at stance, hand position on the ball, body position, proper body movement; whether the ball goes in the basket or not is of little importance to the teacher. They focus on the steps necessary to make the shot, which is what the child needs to learn. Once they learn the proper technique they will begin to make more and more of their attempts.

Instruction through lessons should not always come from the parent. The parent's role is to support the child and be mom or dad, not coach. In any sport you can ask around to find a qualified person to give your child lessons. There could be local high school or college athletes or coaches who could be very helpful in teaching your son or daughter proper technique. Also there are often camps in the summer where kids can get much useful instruction.

Coaching Your Own Child

If you do end up coaching your child, here are some tips. First of all, when practice is over, transform instantly back into mom or dad; do not continue the practice in the car on the way home or once you are at home. The next thing you should do is treat your kid the same as you treat the other kids. Many parents who coach their kids are much harder on their own kids than the other kids. They do not want to show favoritism, so they are tougher on their own child. Other coaches clearly favor their own children.

For the person who coaches his or her child, the next thing to remember is, don't try to teach your kid technique. Your child does not listen to you. (I hate to be the one that breaks the news to you.) No matter how good you were in sports, or how knowledgeable you are about sports, you are still mom or dad. But there are a couple ways to address this issue.

The first way comes from Nort Thornton, the Head Swim Coach at Cal now and while I was coaching there too. Nort's son Richard made the 1980 Olympic team and swam for Nort at Cal. I asked Nort how he coached his son. His reply was, "When I wanted Richard to do something, I told the kid next to him to do it. I always made sure Richard could hear what I was telling the other swimmer. I knew if I told him directly, he probably wouldn't listen. Richard often came up to me and said, 'You know what you were telling Joe? I tried it and it worked for me.'" Richard never knew that Joe was probably doing it right to start with, but Nort knew that he could not directly tell Richard what to do.

Another option is to have your assistant coaches teach the skill. Break the team into two groups and have your assistant coach work with the group your child is in. All of you should work on the same skill. Prep your

> For the person who coaches his or her child, the next thing to remember is, don't try to teach your kid technique. Your child does not listen to you. (I hate to be the one that breaks the news to you.) No matter how good you were in sports, or how knowledgeable you are about sports, you are still mom or dad. But there are a couple ways to address this issue.

assistant by telling him or her ahead of time that your child needs to work on the skill you will be practicing.

Another option for teaching your child would be to have another child on the team demonstrate the skill, then to have everyone watch and try to copy the skill. This does not necessarily need to be done by the best player. While coaching, I often used the kids who were not the stars to demonstrate a skill. They were also doing it right and being the demonstrator helped their self-esteem.

> If you push your child too much in sports two things will probably happen. First of all, your children will resent you; secondly they will probably quit as a teenager—the time when they need sports the most.

Be Careful About Pushing Your Child

If you push your child too much in sports two things will probably happen. First of all, your children will resent you; secondly they will probably quit as a teenager—the time when they need sports the most. It should be your goal as a parent to have your child participating in sports in high school—not excelling—just participating.

Recently, while I was speaking with the parents of middle school children, one parent told me about her sixth grade daughter. Her daughter was in the highest level of soccer, a league higher than the Select League. For her daughter, soccer practice started with a three-mile run. The next part of practice was about an hour and a half of scrimmaging and drills. They finished off practice with a two-mile run. A sixth grader doing this type of training is prone to serious injury and more than likely will burn out when it comes time to play in high school. As a parent, be careful about allowing your child to do this type of training at such an early age.

During the same conversation another parent asked if I thought it was all right for her to force her child to do a sport in eighth or ninth grade. My answer was absolutely "Yes." From seventh to ninth grade is the time to push and from sixth grade and younger is the time to hold them back. There is a very fine and delicate line here. If you push too soon, you will not be able to push later. You need to know when to push and when to back off. Do not always push your children, or your children will think that you are unreasonable and that you don't understand what they are going through so they will quit.

Life Lessons

One thing I have spoken about for years is that sports are a great learning ground. The cornerstone to my philosophy of sports is that sports provide a place to learn the lessons of life. Indeed, General Omar N. Bradley, speaking about sports, said "No extracurricular endeavor I know of could better prepare a soldier for the battlefield."*

Here are some of the lessons I feel your child can learn by participating in sports that will help them with their life:

1. Kids need to be able to set and plan goals; this is what sports are all about. The first set of goals could be hitting or kicking a ball. Goals could come in the form of learning how to swim, skate, or make a basket. The longer your child stays in sports, the better he or she gets at goal setting. All Division One college athletes are experts on goal setting; they could not have gotten to the college level without setting goals.

Let's look at the process for basketball players. As youngsters their goal is to learn how to dribble and how to make a shot. Quickly they progress into getting competent at ball handling and rebounding. Their next goals are to learn plays. As

---

*Bradley, Omar N. *A General's Life*. New York: Simon & Schuster, 1983.

they get older their goals can be both personal and team goals. Personal goals are points scored, rebounds, assists, and blocked shots; team goals are often around making the playoffs. If they are playing in high school, they have many years of solid goal setting behind them. These experiences help with the goal of getting into colleges, studying for finals, planning a career, or saving money. Young athletes learn how to transfer the skill of goal setting in sports to setting goals in their lives.

2. Young athletes learn how to deal with setbacks. All Division One college athletes have experienced setbacks during their careers. By the time they get to college, they have all had either bad games or bad seasons. For a basketball player, chances are by the time they are playing in college they have made a shot to win a game and they have missed a shot and lost the game. They have learned how to deal with both situations. They have learned to keep on plugging away and not get caught up in the ups and downs of sports or life. Many coaches will say the best athletes are the ones who deal with setbacks the best. The athletes who cannot deal with setbacks often quit. If things are going great they are fine; if not, they don't know how to handle it. They can't deal with their own failure in sports and in turn can't deal with failure in life. Think of a teenager who breaks up with his or her girlfriend or boyfriend; this is a traumatic experience for many teens. Having the experience of dealing with setbacks in sports can help them get through life stressors—like the ups and downs of a relationship. Sean Killion, a member of the 1992 Olympic Swimming Team, said in 2005, "Learning how to deal with setbacks in swimming has helped me deal with setbacks over the past thirteen years."

3. Kids can learn how to get along better with others. It seems now many kids want to be superstars; they only want to play if they can be the stars of the team. This is an unfortunate situation. One of the good things about sports is they can help kids learn cooperation with others. Over time kids learn that

105

they do not have to like the people on their team—it helps—but they can learn to play and get along with others they may not particularly like. How is this important in life? Think of your work environment. You may not like everyone, but hopefully you have the skills to get along with those you do not like.

4. Kids learn time management skills. This may not happen until your child does sports in high school. When children are doing a sport in high school they have to use time management skills; there are simply too many things for them to do. Hopefully they learn to get their homework done, get some rest, and make it to practice and games, as well as have time to socialize. Also, high schools have grade requirements, which require young athletes to keep their grades up so they are eligible to play.

5. Sports can keep your kids out of trouble. I feel it is incredibly important for your kids to do a sport in high school. This is a time when without structure, kids can get into trouble. I have heard many people say when they quit sports in high school, their drug use escalated. I am not saying sports will keep your kids off drugs, but if you have practice at 8:00 A.M. on Saturday, chances are that you are getting to bed early Friday night. Sports provide a structure that can keep your kids occupied in healthy ways.

6. Sports can help your child's self-esteem. Teenage years are a time of big swings in a child's self-esteem. If they are doing a sport in high school, they are usually physically fit and feel good about themselves in at least this one area of their lives.

7. Sports can help your kids meet new friends. Through sports kids see the world beyond their own school. They often get to meet kids from other schools, kids whom they may not have met any other way. Sports help broaden their horizons, and travel exposes them to different types of people.

8. Sports help kids stay in shape. Weight has become a serious issue with kids. Many schools no longer have physical education classes. Today's kids now sit around and surf the net or play computer games, and their diet is terrible. Sports can help kids learn a proper diet and help them keep physically fit. When they get older and want to either stay in shape or lose weight, they know how to work out and know the benefits of working out.

9. Kids learn about the quick fix in sports. Often people look for the quick fix in life; sports teaches kids there is no quick fix. Kids see superstars and want to be like them. The longer they are in sports, the more they realize how much effort it takes to keep climbing the ladder in sports. Later in life this helps them with everything from losing weight to work. They learn that to reach their goals, they must go through a process. They learn there is no quick fix and to approach their own problems more realistically.

Thirteen years after Olympian Sean Killion's swimming career ended he said, "When I think about it, I learned more from sport than anything else in my life. Sports prepared me for the real world. I learned life is not a linear progression up. I developed coping skills through sports that I will use for the rest of my life."

Participation

Participation comes first. Your child must first participate— competition comes after participation. I have had kids come to see me who have been diagnosed with ADHD, attention deficit hyperactivity disorder. I suggest to the parent that the kid get involved in sports because most times the kids are not active in sports. When the parent asks, "What sport should they do?" I say, "One like soccer, with a lot of running." This child needs an outlet; soccer is a great way to tire out the child with ADHD. How hyperactive is little Johnny going to be after playing two thirty or forty-five minute halves of soccer? I say try sports before medication.

Many parents get upset because their kids are not focused when playing a sport. Once, when my daughter and I were at a park, a soccer game was going on. I went over and watched for a few minutes. When I came back, I told my daughter, "Those people are crazy." She asked what I was talking about. I said, "Look over at the sidelines and see if you can guess which one is the coach." There were probably ten parents running up and down the field telling their kids what to do. The kids looked dazed and confused—they were only eight years old.

The longer your child stays in sports the more he or she will learn how to compete. The initial task is to get your kid on a team. Once this is accomplished, competition may be a few years away, but it will come.

You Never Know How Good Your Child Can Be

Most people are aware Michael Jordan was cut from his ninth grade basketball team. Think of it, Michael Jordan, probably the greatest basketball player of all time, was told in ninth grade he was not good enough to be on his school's freshman team. Michael Jordan could have given up basketball forever. The point is, when he was in ninth grade, his incredible talent was not overwhelming anyone. Former NBA stars Bob Cousy and Bob Pettit were both cut from their high school basketball teams their freshman and sophomore years. After leading his team to the Louisiana State High School Championship, Pettit signed with LSU. During his four years at LSU Pettit grew another five inches. This is why it is important to think about the long term for your child. You should not worry how good your kids are when they are eight, ten, or even twelve years old.

Make sure your children are participating in at least one, though hopefully more than one sport, when they are young. They should be doing some sport most of the year; they do not need to specialize at an early age. If kids become well-rounded athletes when young, they will have more options when they specialize in one sport when they are older.

Every college coach can tell you about athletes who did not bloom until they got to college. If you can keep your children involved in sports long enough, you can have a chance to see how good they can possibly be. The key to all this, obviously, is to make sure they stay involved in sports by slowly bringing them along. Michael Jordan, Bob Cousy and Bob Pettit all practiced very hard after they were cut from their high school basketball teams. The work ethic each of them established after being cut in high school is what helped make them NBA superstars.

Fun

Make sure the kids are having fun in sports; remember fun for a young kid may mean going to get ice cream after the game. I believe the definition of fun changes over time. Many young children do not care if they win or lose and as a parent you should not care either. I remember watching a young kid leaving a Little League baseball game; his dad arrived and asked, "Who won?" The child replied, "I don't know." The dad said, "Go find out." The kid then went and asked the coach who won, then returned to his dad and said, "We won, dad." The dad then asked, "What was the score?" The kid replied, "I don't know." The dad said, "Go find out. They beat you guys by three runs last game." This kid did not care about the score; he was having fun playing with his friends after the game. The kids were playing basketball with a baseball glove acting as the ball, something only kids can do. For this child the basketball game with his teammates was fun. The more a parent focuses on winning and losing, the more your kid will do the same.

When kids get older fun becomes making the all star team or traveling to out-of-town competitions. I remember when I was swimming in college; we had to be back at school on December

26th to train. School did not start until January 15th, so we had three weeks on campus all alone. This was our very hard training time. All we did was wake up, eat, swim, eat, take a nap, swim, eat, and then play either Hearts or Risk in the evening. If we went to a movie, we were often the only ones in the theater. While this was going on, we were all convinced this was the worst experience of our lives. Years later, we realized it actually was a very fun time. We were hanging out with our friends and had no worries about anything other than swimming. You may not always know you are having fun at the time it is happening. The fellowship and camaraderie with teammates is often a big part of the fun in sports.

> You may not always know you are having fun at the time it is happening. The fellowship and camaraderie with teammates is often a big part of the fun in sports.

When a kid gets to high school fun is being on the team and getting attention at school. The next level of fun is getting a scholarship to college; also it is fun to go to the Olympics or on to a professional career. However, it is important to remember that the initial fun in sports is just being on the team with your friends and the outcome is not important at all.

No Autopsy

Don't do post mortems on your child's games. A post mortem is when parents dissect the game with their kids. They feel they need to break down the game and tell their kid what they thought of the game. This can be done a little, but only for a few minutes after the game. For many parents, the kid's game is the topic of conversation for way too long. You should ask if they had fun, then take the lead from them. If they want to talk more about the game then do so; if you feel they do not want to talk about their game, then let it go. This is especially true when your child makes a big mistake in a game. The time to talk about the mistake may be four or five days later. You may want to be a little reassuring, but often they are in so much emotional pain that they do not want to talk at all. The best thing to do is to ask them if they feel like you are talking too much about their games.

Don't Live Through Your Children

You should not try to live your life though your children; this is a sure recipe for a disaster. Parents must learn to separate their child's successes from their own. If their child scores the winning goal, don't try to take any credit, like saying, "Good thing we worked on your shot." If your child is the greatest player in your area, be as anonymous as possible. You should be supportive and encouraging but don't steal their thunder.

Think of it from the kid's point of view. If they do badly, it's their fault; if they do great, it's because you helped them. This is a no-win situation for the kids. This is why many kids with overbearing parents either quit sports or end up resenting their parents. Your child will need a lot of therapy if you keep trying to live out your dreams through them.

Be a Role Model

You should act the way you want your kids to act. If you do not want your kid yelling at the referee, then you should not. Good sportsmanship comes from the parents first, then the coach. You should be a role model of sportsmanship; do not expect professional players to be role models for your children. Do not yell at the opposing players or coaches. Make sure your children shake hands with or high five their

> Think of it from the kid's point of view. If they do badly, it's their fault; if they do great, it's because you helped them. This is a no-win situation for the kids.

opponents after each game. I know of a high school basketball game where the coach took his team off the floor with over a minute left to play in the game. His team was down by ten points and he didn't like the calls the referees had made during the game. When he pulled his team one of his players went and shook hands with each of the players on the other team. This is what good sportsmanship is about; your child needs to show good sportsmanship in spite of other parents, teammates, and some coaches. Also, there should be no trash talk.

As far as modeling goes, you should take your young son or daughter to a high school game of their favorite sport; if you have a local college, you could take them to see their sporting events. It is very important for young children, especially girls, to see where sports can take them. Going to a high school game when you are ten or twelve years old can show you the excitement that high school sports have to offer.

Quitting

I believe that quitting during the season is rarely an option. About the only time a child should quit during the season is if the coach is abusive. This comes in the form of verbal abuse; a verbally abusive coach can harm a kid's self-esteem for a long time. If the coach is detrimental to your child's emotional health, you have some options. First of all, you can talk to the coach, never in front of any of the kids on the team, and voice your concerns. Secondly, many sports have a league office. You can contact the commissioner of your league and state your concerns about the coach. If these two things fail and the coach is still abusive, then pull your kid from the sport for the rest of the season. Play with your child during the time he or she would have been at practice with the team. For the two of you, this will be a time of emotional bonding. Many kids allow verbally abusive coaches to end their sporting careers.

Other than a verbally abusive coach there are few reasons to allow a child to quit during the season. You should explain to them at the beginning of the season what joining the team entails. If they agree and later change their mind, too bad, they should stick it out. For many kids wanting to quit is transitory; after a week or so they wish they were back on the team.

If your child does quit one sport, he or she should participate in another sport. My college roommate's ten- and twelve-year-old sons were members of a traveling soccer team. Both boys were not getting much playing time and did not like the coach or the demands of the elite soccer team. They told their parents they wanted to quit. The parents understood their desire to quit and it was somewhat of a relief for them because of the commitment as parents they had to make for their sons to play soccer. However, the parents insisted that once they quit soccer, the boys participate in another sport. Neither of the boys felt competent to start all over in another sport because soccer had taken up all of their time and energy for the past few years. The parents forced the boys to join a swim team, with the understanding that if they did not like swimming after one year, they would both have the option to quit. The parents had been reluctant to make their kids join a swim team, as both parents were swimmers when they were younger.

Although swimming was demanding, the boys approached swimming with the same work ethic they approached soccer. When they joined the swim team, their times were much slower than their peers. However, after a summer of good coaching and hard work, they both had made tremendous progress. They enjoyed the camaraderie of their new team and after a summer of swimming, quitting was not on their minds at all.

Model Emotional Management

You should act the same way if your child's team wins or loses.

I often work with athletes to try to get them to keep a calm exterior; parents should do the same. You should be the rock of support, win or lose. The only time you should express anger at your children is if they are over twelve years old and they are not trying in a game; then you can voice your opinion. Often ten-year-olds go from the swim meet to the baseball game. The only thing you should be concerned with as a parent is, did they try and did they have fun? If your kids are high school athletes, you can't get caught up with the win/loss record. That is the coach's and the team's business, not yours. If you are excited and can't sleep before one of your kid's games, do not tell your children. Model the calmness they need.

Have Reasonable Expectations

You should not expect too much. Often parents expect their kids to be as successful as they are. The parents' hard work has paid off for them; often they expect the same dedication from their ten-year-olds. Let your kids be kids first, students second, and athletes third. Too often parents are yelling at their young kids to focus or get in the game. Simply being on the team, learning the skills, and improving are enough for ten-year-olds and under.

You should not expect your children to get a college scholarship or play professional sports. If it happens, great, but it is not reasonable to even think of a college scholarship until your children are sophomores in high school. College coaches are primarily going to look at how they perform their junior and senior year. Most college coaches like to see athletes who are continuing to improve their last two years of high school.

Parents often want to see the competitive drive in their children that they see in professional and college athletes. This is totally unrealistic. If a child participates, a competitive drive will start to grow and develop. Most high school athletes are competitive. They want to win, and improve their game, although many did not start out this way. Their competitive drive developed over time. If you are a parent, back off. This competitive drive will develop naturally. If you try to instill this drive in your kids at a young age by having them focus on winning, it simply won't work.

I tell my undergraduate students about a study that found there was an $800,000 difference in lifetime earnings between those with a college degree and those without a college degree. Make sure your child finishes college. It is much easier to be a successful professional in the work force than to make millions of dollars as a professional athlete.

Too many parents are spending the equivalent of a year of college tuition at a private college to try to fulfill their dream of having their son or daughter make the Olympic team. Success in school should be more of a priority than success as an athlete.

Weaknesses

Every athlete has strengths and weaknesses. As a parent you should not discourage your children from trying to improve on the weak areas of their sport. Many athletes try to hide their weaknesses. This is a natural thing to do. The problem is that many athletes do not improve on their weaknesses. In practice they only work on their strengths. Think of tennis. If a player has a great forehand but his backhand needs improvement, how does he approach this? Does he spend a certain amount of time working on his backhand each day? By attempting to hide their weaknesses, many athletes do not spend enough time trying to improve the weak areas of their game.

As a parent you should not encourage your children to gloss over the weak aspects of their play. Some parents will say to a baseball player, "Don't swing at a curve ball, you can't hit them anyway." Parents will tell young tennis players to run around on their backhand. Running around means trying to get into position to hit a forehand instead of hitting a backhand. If your children focus only on their strengths and do not work to improve their weaknesses, they become stagnant as athletes. By allowing your children to have weaknesses, "You hit thirty percent of your backhands today, last match you hit twenty-five; your backhand is getting better," over time they will see their weaker areas not as a weakness, but as an area that they need to work on and improve. Too many parents encourage their kids to work on their strengths, and their weaknesses get ignored.

Focusing only on the strong aspects of their game is how a young athlete's negative self-talk starts to develop. Kids say to themselves, "My backhand sucks," rather than, "I need to work on my backhand." It is not like a tennis player is born with a bad backhand; by seeing it as a skill they need to work on, they can measure their improvement. Otherwise they tend to view a weakness in an on-off fashion. They think, "My backhand was all right today," or, "My backhand was terrible today." It is almost as if by some mystical reason their backhand either works or it does not work. They need to see that they are the agents of change and that their backhand will improve the more time they spend working to improve it.

Recently, I was speaking with a NCAA Division One basketball coach. I asked him what advice he would pass on to high school or junior college basketball players. He said, "They should work on their weaknesses every day, because once they get into college, the opposition will identify and exploit their weakness. If they have trouble going to their left, they should work on going to their left every day. In high school a player can often get by with many weaknesses; in college the level of play is so much greater that opposing coaches and players will spot a weakness and attack the opponent constantly where they are weak. I know no one likes to work on his or her weaknesses, but it is something I focus on in my practices daily. How would you like to be the player the opposition tries to foul at the end of the game because they know you are not a good free throw shooter?" He added, "When I am recruiting a player of course I look at what they can do, but I also look at what they cannot do. I want to see how much coaching it is going to take to get them to improve on their weaknesses. Too many high school and junior college players look at their basic statistics only, scoring, rebounding, assists. When recruiting, I am looking at the total player. I take note of his ability to move, pass, defend, his attitude and self-confidence. I look at the player and think if he was on the opposing team, how would I attack him? I am amazed at the number of high school players who focus on their scoring alone. The pace of the game is so much faster at the Division One level, a player needs to be able to do much more than score."

Burn-Out

It is the parents' responsibility to prevent their children from burning out. Somewhere along the way I heard the saying, "When the fruit is ripe, you pick it." What is happening in sports all across the country is that fruit is being picked too soon. In other words, we are trying to get these great results from our ten- to twelve-year-olds and by the time the kids hit age fifteen or sixteen, when they should be picked, they are already burned out and rotten.

As a parent you should hold your children back when they are young. Do not let them play for teams that are demanding an unreasonable commitment before they are in seventh grade. Prior to seventh grade they should be playing many different sports. If your children learn how to be successful at one sport, it is easy to transfer the skills to another sport when they are older. Most kids are not exposed to sports like volleyball, crew, track and field, field hockey, or lacrosse (except on the East Coast) until they are older. If your children learn the basic skills in sports, like hand-eye coordination, running, throwing, and catching, they can transfer the sport skills to a new sport when the time comes.

The sport where I see the most problems is soccer. Kids are playing in select and all star leagues almost their whole lives. By the time they turn sixteen they want to try something else because they are sick of soccer. If your children are good athletes prior to sixth grade and participate in sports, when the time comes they can progress quickly. As a parent, keep in mind that your child's sport career is like a long distance race. If you start out too fast you have nothing left at the end of the race. Your first goal as a parent is to make sure your child is still in the race at the end. No success, no matter how great, before the age of twelve means anything in the long run.

> No success, no matter how great, before the age of twelve means anything in the long run.

As a parent, if you hold your children back when they are in elementary school, then push them when they are in seventh or eighth grade, they will do much better in the long run than children that have been pushed all along. Of course the problem here is that they will not be as good as the other kids when they are in seventh grade. But if they have always been active in sports, as they should be, it will not take long to catch up to and even pass the other kids. Speaking to parent groups, I have had parents verbally attack me when I have made this statement. Because there is so much competition to make the middle school team, parents feel they have to push their kids in grade school. In the long run pushing your child in grade school does not work.

Burn-out comes from someone not improving or having

fun. You don't see athletes who are improving and having a great time decide to quit. If kids are pushed from elementary school on, by the time they hit high school they are not improving anymore. They are tired of the monotony and drudgery of the same old thing, day in and day out. Since there is no improvement, they decide to quit so they can hang out with their friends.

Roque (pronounced Rock) Santos swam for us at Cal. In high school Roque played football and basketball and he swam. He was a walk-on at Cal, meaning he did not have a swimming scholarship. Nort Thornton, the head coach, had coached Roque's older brother Dave, and knew Roque had the talent to develop into a great swimmer. Nort was not concerned with how fast Roque was coming into Cal; he saw Roque's potential. Roque turned into an outstanding swimmer and made the 1992 Olympic team. He improved all throughout his college career.

Roque's 1992 Olympic teammate, Sean Killion, said when he was fourteen years old, his swim coach, Hugh Merkle, asked Sean to commit to swimming for the summer. Up to this time, Sean was still participating in three sports. Coach Merkle had told Sean for the past three years, "When the time comes for you to commit full time to swimming, I'll ask you to commit, but I don't want anyone to commit until they can physically and emotionally handle the workload involved." Coach Merkle asked Sean to give swimming a try the summer before ninth grade. That summer Sean qualified for the Junior National Swimming Championships in four events. Sean and Coach Merkle then sat down and came up with a four-year plan for Sean. This included a gradual build-up in training yardage and intensity. Four years later, as a high school senior, Sean placed third in the National Championships.

There are many success stories out there of kids who were not superstars when they were twelve years old. Stop and look around at the former MVP of the league that your ten- to twelve-year-old is in. See where these MVPs ended up when they were eighteen years old. Yes, some went on to bigger and better things; they were always great athletes and this continued, but I am quite certain that for many of the stars of the ten-to-twelve age group, that was their glory time. This is a tragic situation and is the cause of burn-out. Wait until the fruit is ripe, and then pick it.

Evaluating a High School Coach

Often parents question if they should have their child transfer to another high school to play for a different coach. Although recruiting is illegal in high school athletics, it is a common practice in many areas of the country. Many high school coaches are good at selling their program. However, a good salesman does not always make a good coach. It is a common saying in college athletics that, "Recruiting is everything." But the ability to recruit good athletes is only one aspect of a good coach.

When choosing a coach, parents need to look at the long-term results the coach has produced. Recently, someone asked me if I thought he should have his son, a high school basketball player, change schools. I said, "Tell me about your son's coach." The feedback I got was that the coach had been at the school for over twenty years. Over the years the coach had some winning teams, but no player from his teams ever went on to play Division One basketball. The coach often blamed individual kids for the team's failures. The coach claimed he was a strict disciplinarian, saying that if the kids couldn't handle his rules they could "pack up their gear and go home." The coach often yelled at the kids because they did not hustle off the court during a substitution. At times, he would belittle players in front of their teammates. The players feared that if they did not follow the coach's strict rules then they would lose their playing time. The coach's style was more about enforcing his will on the team, rather than teaching the kids how to become better basketball players.

The parent told me that during a game, most of the players on the team were constantly looking over toward the coach. The players seemed uptight and scared; there was no flow in their game. The players were paralyzed by their fear of the coach's wrath.

Unfortunately, because many parents have no experience in sports, it is often hard for them to tell an incompetent coach from a good coach. When playing for a good coach, the players improve. It should be obvious to parents if they notice improvement in their own child or their child's teammates. Anyone can yell. It takes a competent teacher to help guide and nurture young athletes to help them develop.

The parent told me that the coach had the team stay after one of their losses and run sprints. The coach felt that the reason the team lost the game was because the players were not tough enough and felt some extra running would toughen the players up. While the players were running up and down the court, the coach was calling the players derogatory names and yelling at them. The parent reported that the coach often had the players do such punishment type drills.

The reality of the situation was that the team lost the game because the other team was a better team with a better coach. No coach ever wants to admit that he or she was out-coached. This coach's explanation for all of his team's losses always was that the other team had more talent, or that his players did not play hard enough. The coach never looked at his own role in his team's losses. The coach created an environment for his team that stifled his players' ability to play basketball. The players never relaxed on the court; they played uptight and rigid. Thus, their confidence in their own ability never grew and developed. In the coach's mind his team lost because they needed more hard work and discipline.

Discipline is very important in coaching. A good coach knows how to control and discipline his or her team. However, there is a difference between discipline and punishment. Discipline helps keep a team in line. Discipline makes players accountable for their actions, both to themselves and to the team. Some coaches lock the doors when practice starts as a way to make sure everyone is on time, feeling that locking the doors is a way to instill the discipline of getting to practice on time. Although many coaches never lock doors, some successful coaches do use this approach.

Punishment is different. Punishment is punitive and disrespectful. Punishment is humiliating. If someone breaks a team rule, he or she should be disciplined, not humiliated. The difference between discipline and punishment is how the consequences are enforced. Having an athlete do extra work is not necessarily punishment. How the extra work is presented to the athlete often determines the difference between discipline and punishment. No coach on any level should disrespect or humiliate an athlete.

The parent told me that the high school coach his son played for often disrespected his athletes both during practice and games. I explained that there is a big difference between punishment work and conditioning work. There is nothing wrong with working athletes hard. When John Wooden led UCLA to ten NCAA basketball titles, his team was the best conditioned team in the country. If a coach has a player or a team do extra work for any reason, the extra work should have a point. John Wooden told his team that no matter which team they played, he wanted the UCLA players to know they were in better shape than their opponents were. However, Wooden also focused on and taught the fundamentals of basketball every day. Many of the former UCLA players say playing for John Wooden was like taking a college class in basketball. John Wooden's teams worked very hard, but he was never disrespectful toward his athletes.

Demanding, hard work is what sports is all about, but if the coach is not knowledgeable enough about the sport and is disrespectful to the athletes, then the athletes will resent the coach. If the athletes do not see the payoff for their hard work they think, it's not worth it. The athletes will rebel against the coach and undermine the coach's authority. A coach that can combine the hard work with proper educational instruction is the coach you want to have working with your children. The coach may discipline your child, but he or she will not humiliate your child.

As in the case above, there are times when it is in your child's best interest to switch high schools. Your child needs to be in an environment that will help him or her develop as a complete athlete. In the long run, a disrespectful coach does not produce confident athletes. Regardless of an athlete's talent, without confidence he or she will never reach his or her full potential. Children need both physical and emotional skills to succeed in sports. A good coach nurtures both skills. A great coach is one who can not only teach the sport but also instill self-confidence in his or her athletes. No athlete succeeds without a combination of physical and emotional skills.

CHAPTER 7

Fred—High School Basketball

F red came to see me during his senior year in high school. He had been playing basketball his whole life and now played for his high school team. The season had just started. Fred and his parents were already concerned with the level of his play.

Fred usually played small forward or, at times, number two guard. He had played in a summer league with the same players who were on his high school team. His play had been very erratic lately. One game he would score twenty points; the next four games he would not score twenty points combined. He had never been a starter for the team, but was recently demoted from being the sixth man to being about the eighth man on the team. His coach was frustrated with Fred's inconsistency and recently cut Fred's playing time. Fred's school played in a tough conference; many games were close and often played to sellout crowds.

During our first session, Fred said he got frustrated when his shots "were not falling." He described himself as a pure shooter; he felt his role on the team was to score, especially to make three-point shots. Once in the game, if Fred missed his first three shots in a row, he would often quickly become discouraged. The coach also saw him as a streak shooter. Often, when the team was behind, the coach would put Fred in and, at times, Fred would make his first three shots and bring the team back into the game. If Fred missed his first three shots; the coach would pull him from the game. Both the coach and Fred would figure he was not on that game.

Fred told me that if he missed a shot he would look over at the coach. With each shot Fred missed, the coach showed more irritation and disappointment. Fred said it was usually after three misses that the coach would look down the bench for a substitute for Fred. The coach seemed to play his substitutes a few minutes at a time, to see if any of them were on that game. Thus, Fred became very self-conscious, timid, tentative, and fearful on the court.

In the first session I worked to redefine Fred's game. We broke his game down into different parts—defense, rebounding, ball handling and passing, blocked shots, steals, free throws, and shooting. Seen in this light, shooting was only one part of his game, not his whole game. I felt that if I could get him to focus on other aspects of his game, he would not live and die by his shot. He wrote my comments down and I asked him to evaluate each area of his game daily after practice. I wanted Fred to give himself a score from one to ten on each aspect of his game. Furthermore, I wanted him to try to work on each aspect during practice, before our meeting next week. I asked that when we met the next week, he report the scores he gave himself during the week in each area.

Frequently, I tell my graduate students that one task they often face is to help take pressure off athletes. Fred put a tremendous amount of pressure on himself; he felt that he had to produce points the instant he entered a game. He felt he was not allowed to miss any shots and had to be on. His coach reinforced this belief too. When Fred was on, the coach played him; if Fred was off, he might only get in the game in the second half for a few minutes to see if he was on then. By having Fred focus on other aspects of his game, I was taking pressure off of his shooting. I felt this could help Fred relax and play better.

For our next session Fred came in with the scores he had given himself. There was improvement in a few areas. The key thing I was looking for was taking place. Fred was now aware of the other aspects of his game besides shooting. I was not interested in the actual scores he gave himself. I wanted his awareness and focus to shift from his shooting to these other areas of his game.

Fred had some insights while reporting these things to me. One thing he said was, "My defense has not been good lately; I used to take pride in my defense. I realize I have not been aggressive on defense at all lately." When his shot was off, his total body posture on the court changed; he slumped over and his whole game would fall apart. Fred was beginning to see the importance of focusing on all areas of his game.

The next issue we addressed was his shooting percentage. Fred thought when he was "on," he should make every shot. I had him tell me what he thought his shooting percentage should be from the floor, foul line, and three-point range. He began to realize that three-point shots are not high percentage shots. This seemed like it should be obvious. He was a senior in high school, quite smart, yet he had not conceptualized the likelihood of making 40% of his three-point shots. By this I mean, it seemed a bit of a revelation to him that he would be missing 60% of these shots. I wanted Fred to have a realistic view of what he was trying to accomplish.

For our next session Fred came in with the scores he had given himself. There was improvement in a few areas. The key thing I was looking for was taking place. Fred was now aware of the other aspects of his game besides shooting. I was not interested in the actual scores he gave himself. I wanted his awareness and focus to shift from his shooting to these other areas of his game.

Fred was a good free throw shooter. Last year he made four free throws in the last two minutes to help his team win a close game. He knew that his team often lost games because of poor free throw shooting. He wanted to continue to improve his free throw shooting and averaged over 85% from the free throw line.

Next, we went over game type scenarios. I often do this in detail. I had Fred tell me how many shots he should take from the field in each game. His initial reply was "about ten." Of these ten shots, about five or six of them would be from the three-point line. This means if he were two for five, or three for six from the three point line, he would be playing well. We then went over warm-up. Fred often just shot during warm-up. Many counselors who work with athletes are constantly concerned about crossing the line between coaching and counseling. Going over how an athlete warms up is not coaching in my book, nor is talking about what shots to take and when to take them. Teaching a shooting technique does cross over the line into coaching.

After we examined Fred's warm-up pattern, we worked to implement a new one. The team did their regular warm-up routine, then the players were allowed to shoot, stretch, or work on whatever they wanted to work on. Fred said during the free time he often shot from behind the three-point line. We came up with a new plan of action. Remembering the old coaching adage "Nothing succeeds like success," I wanted Fred to be successful in warm-ups so I had him start by taking some shots close to the basket. He said these were never a problem for him; thus he did not feel the need to work on close range shots during warm-up. I wanted Fred to make easy shots first, establish a rhythm, and then gradually move out to the three-point line.

Fred began to try to do this during warm-up for practice too. These close shots only took a few extra minutes and helped build Fred's confidence. Also, this way his shot was not limited to his three-point shot. I talked about Fred having an arsenal of weapons, the three-point shot being one of the weapons. I asked Fred to talk about the other weapons he possessed and I could see a light go on in his head as he began to describe his options when he had the ball. "I can drive to the basket; actually, I should be driving more. I love to drive. Also, I can stop and pop, which is my mom's favorite shot. And, of course, I can shoot the three." The stop and pop is when he would start to drive to the goal, stop quickly, and shoot. These were just three options; he began to see his option of passing the ball at any point while he had the ball.

Prior to this Fred saw his options as shoot, or don't shoot. Usually he shot even when he did not have a good scoring opportunity. As Fred began to see his options, he started to feel more in control when he had the ball.

One other thing I usually do in my early work with athletes is go over their best and worst performances. Fred said, "I had a game where I had two points in the first half and ended up with twenty-four points for the game." In his worst game he said, "I went 0 for everything—really like 0 points for 10 shots. It was a summer game; otherwise, the coach would have pulled me."

My reason for going over both best and worst performances is because, as I see it, I often do not need to teach someone a new skill. They have had success; they need to learn how to take their success, identify what went right, and work to make what they did successfully an ingrained behavior. Fred could score and he could play well; he just was not able to play consistently. I just needed to get him to take his success and make it a regular occurrence. It is much easier to work with someone who has had some success than it is to work with someone who has not had any success at all. Think of golf. It is much easier to get someone who can shoot around par to do that on a consistent basis than it is to work with someone who has never broken one hundred and get them to shoot par. Fred had the tools; we just needed to keep them sharp.

Following this theme, we looked at what went right in Fred's best performances. His description of his play in these games was that he was in the zone, or "I didn't have to think; I couldn't miss." Like many athletes Fred was not able to pinpoint what was going right; he was simply happy to be playing great. That was enough for him. We went back over the game when he scored twenty-two points in the second half and I had him break down exactly what was happening during the game. He began to see how his first few shots tremendously impacted his confidence. During the first half, he went one for five, missing three three-point shots. He felt lethargic; the coach saw he was not on and Fred sat out the rest of the half.

During the second half, Fred came in and made two two-point shots, had a steal and a lay-up, then hit a three-point shot. In just a few minutes he had scored nine points, then he was off to the races. He said he felt light and that everything flowed. He made his next two three-point shots; however, overall for the game this made him three for six from the three-point line. In Fred's mind, he hit all his three-point shots up to that point; it was as if the first half was a whole other game.

This led to us exploring Fred's confidence. He said his confidence waxed and waned with his ability to score. Also, the coach's confidence in him followed this same pattern. The coach reinforced that Fred was either on or off. I began to have Fred explain to me the parts of his game where he had the most confidence—other than his shot. This shifted his focus to other aspects of his game. The key task now was to get Fred to maintain his confidence if he happened to miss his first couple of shots.

The next issue that came up was pressure—especially from Fred's parents. Fred's dad had been his basketball coach in grade school; they had a successful team and Fred often played great. His dad would want to sit down with Fred after games and go over Fred's play; his dad would point out all the mistakes Fred made. When Fred scored twenty-four points, his dad's response was, "You could have had thirty points."

This is a common approach parents often take; they feel that they should push their kids, that their kids should never be satisfied. The problem with this approach is that the kids don't let the good things sink in. What I mean by this is, by constantly telling kids what they could have done better, the kids don't look at what they did well. Their confidence does not grow. Looking back on their performance they focus on "What I didn't do right," which perpetuates not looking at where and why they had success. By not knowing what they did that created the success, they become inconsistent.

Fred's dad felt like he was helping Fred; he felt like he was giving Fred some extra coaching that he was not getting from his basketball coach. His dad was critical of the coach's style and felt like he could do a better job coaching the team. The thing was, his dad was probably right; he may have been a better coach than the high school coach was. However, this was not helpful for Fred's play or confidence.

The other issue here is that these review sessions with dad had no time frame; they would start during the drive home and continue during dinner—with some diagrams and plays drawn. Then, if something came to him later, Dad would say to Fred, "One other thing I forgot to say was…"

Fred felt like he had no break. His mom was encouraging, before the game saying something like, "How many points are you going to score tonight?" This seems cute, but how was Fred to answer that question? Fred did not know what to say or do with his parents because during basketball season his house turned into a basketball school.

I felt like it was time for a "parentectomy." I had to come up with a way to remove the negative impact Fred's parents were having on him. Fred felt like he never had any down time. He had to deal with his coaches at practice and his parents when he got home, and he did not know how to deal with the pressure from his parents. Many kids simply quit at this stage. They don't really want to quit; they simply want the pressure to go away. Also, this is a time when one hears the term "burn-out." Burn-out is the accumulation of stress on these kids. It is not necessarily that the kids hate the sport; they want the pressure to go away. Sports often become too demanding for kids because the parents are an added source of stress.

When I suggested to Fred that we come up with a way to cut the comments from his parents, he perked up instantly. I asked him, "How could we do this?" His reply was, "I have no idea, but I like the concept." I suggested that he tell his parents that they were not allowed to comment on how basketball was going. Many people working with athletes look toward empowering the athletes. They feel that having the athletes do these things for themselves helps empower them. Thus, the athlete takes more responsibility for his or her success. I understand this concept; however, we did not really have time for Fred to talk to his parents on his own.

I asked Fred if it would be easier for him to talk to his parents himself, or say, "Tom told me to say...." He said he liked the second approach. This was okay with me, as I wanted the problem addressed, and I did not care how it was done at the time. Time was our critical factor; had I been working with Fred prior to his senior year, I may have chosen another route.

An interesting thing happened when Fred told his parents they were not allowed to comment about basketball—they were very receptive. At this stage they were willing to do whatever was necessary to help Fred. We allowed his dad to have about fifteen minutes to half an hour to comment after a game, but that was all. If he thought of something later, it had to wait. His mom's attitude was great; she brought some levity to the situation. She would ask, "Is it okay if I wish you good luck? I don't want to put pressure on you."

The results were almost instantaneous. Fred's game got much better and he moved back up to his position as sixth man. He got more playing time and worked to improve all areas of his game. He now felt like he was ready for the team's upcoming big tournament. The team would be away for about a week and there were many quality teams that would be attending the tournament. Also, many parents made the trip to the tournament too, making it a group vacation. The previous year Fred's team made it to the semi-finals. They were quite happy with this outcome and hoped for a repeat performance this season.

Even I was shocked when Fred sat down for our next session. He said, "I played great. Our team won and I was voted MVP of the tournament." This was the first time anyone could remember a sixth man winning the MVP award for the whole tournament. If anyone on Fred's team was ever MVP, it was their top player. Fred had outscored the top player, had more assists, and was seen as the dominant player of his team.

When I asked, "What was your dad's response?" Fred said, "My dad had already left the gym to go back to the hotel. It was totally unexpected." Obviously, both his parents were very pleased, which did wonders for Fred's confidence. Some of his teammates called him by the nickname "MVP" for a few days.

To me, the strange thing was that Fred's playing time did not go up much in the next game. He scored more points than anyone else in the tournament, while playing about 40% **less** time than the starters played. Furthermore, he was not promoted to a starting position; it was as if nothing changed in the coach's mind. To the coach, Fred was still his sixth man—nothing more. I began to question the coach's logic. How could he keep Fred out of the starting lineup the way Fred was playing? In the coach's mind he did not want to mess with the chemistry of the team. I felt my coaching blood begin to boil.

It was not until I went to one of Fred's games that I really understood what was going on with the coach and the team. The person that Fred often substituted for was someone I will call "Beavis." Beavis was a little guy and was the smallest guy on the team, most times, the smallest guy on the court. He rarely shot and most of the time he never even looked to take a shot. However, if there was a loose ball, he was the first to dive for it; he played what looked like very aggressive defense. In short, he was a player that one would say had a lot of hustle. To me, his defense was not effective at all because I noticed he would hustle himself out of many plays, with the guy he was defending not seeming to have a problem scoring on Beavis.

Things really made sense when I looked over at the coach; he was the spitting image of Beavis. Beavis was not his son, but I could guess that the coach had been a player with a big heart and a lot of hustle—and probably not much talent. Beavis was probably his favorite player on the team because he reminded the coach of himself.

The game I went to watch was the second game after the tournament. Fred played a total of four minutes. I knew the frustration I was feeling was small in comparison to what Fred must have been feeling. Because Fred was only in the game for a limited amount of time, he felt like he had to do something spectacular when he got into the game. He knew if he did not score right away, he would soon be right back on the bench.

After talking things over, Fred and I agreed on the next step—Fred needed to talk with the coach. Fred and the coach actually had a good relationship; Fred was also on the tennis team and the basketball coach was the tennis coach as well. Fred and the coach often played tennis together during the summer. The topic of the conversation was going to be playing time. I wanted to make sure Fred was careful when talking with the coach. I knew if he upset the coach, his playing time could be cut even more.

We decided that Fred should approach the coach after school, before practice. This would be a one-on-one conversation in the coach's office. It was best for Fred to talk to the coach alone, rather than get his parents involved. We rehearsed how and what Fred would say to the coach, as I did not want the conversation to turn adversarial. Many times these situations turn out bad because the coach feels like he is being attacked; the coach and the kid end up getting into a shouting match, making the situation much worse. I encouraged Fred to approach the conversation in more of an inquisitive manner—"Coach, what do I need to do to get more playing time?" I told Fred if he wanted to, he could tell the coach he was working with me, as the coach had no knowledge of my involvement with Fred at all.

During our next session Fred reported he and the coach had a good talk; the coach said one reason he was not playing Fred as much was because of Fred's attitude. This was a shock to both Fred and me—his *attitude*? Fred is a happy-go-lucky person. We had been working on getting Fred to relax and not put so much pressure on himself. Since he was relaxed more, the coach saw him as not focused or intense enough. The coach's response was discouraging for both of us because the very things we were working on and were producing results, were now keeping him from getting more playing time. The coach said he would like to see Fred more intense and focused during practice and games.

One thing I tell graduate students is that in their career, every athlete will play for a coach who is an idiot. Fred was now playing for his idiot. I had to be careful not to let my feelings about the coach impact what was happening between Fred and me, or Fred and the coach. I did not tell Fred my feelings about his coach, and throughout our time working together, I don't think Fred ever knew how much I disapproved of his coach.

The coach also stated that since league play was starting he felt more pressure to win, and so he wanted everyone on the team focused for the games. Focused is a term that I feel gets overused in sports.

Being focused does not always result in a great performance. I remember hearing Harris Barton of the San Francisco 49ers being interviewed, talking about playing in the Super Bowl with Joe Montana. There were two minutes left in the game; the 49ers had to go about eighty yards to score. During a time-out, Harris was saying things like, "This is it. This is for the ring. This is what we have worked for all year. Let's get fired up." Joe Montana was relaxed and detached. He said, "Hey Harris, check it out, there is John Candy in the stands." Harris said he was dumbfounded, but sure enough, he looked, and there in the stands was John Candy eating popcorn.

It is my guess that this was Joe Montana's way of saying, "Calm down. Relax. We'll be fine." I have no way of knowing if that was the case, but it sure seemed to work for the 49ers. They came back and won the Super Bowl. However, many high school coaches would argue that Joe Montana was not focused and Harris Barton was really focused. I could not disagree more; both were focused in their own way. What works for one athlete may not work for another. Too often athletes are told to focus the way the coach or their parents want them to be focused, not in a way that actually works for them.

For Fred, being focused meant being calm, loose, and relaxed. We decided that Fred needed to keep an inward relaxation, but an outward look of focus. This way he could keep his game in line and keep the coach off his back.

The next game I could not believe what I saw. Fred was put in toward the end of the first quarter. He made an assist, blocked a shot, made a two-point shot and provided an instant spark for the team. He then had a total mental lapse; he made a terrible pass. The coach instantly pulled him out of the game. This was the coach's pattern. If a player made a mistake, the coach pulled him out, and sent him to the bench to think about it.

Treating athletes this way is a disaster and often happens in basketball. I felt like the coach needed to learn about brain development and the thought process of high school kids—they often make bad decisions. He did not seem to see the instant spark Fred provided for the team and how with Fred in the game, the pace of the game picked up instantly.

When a coach benches a player for a mistake, what the player ends up thinking about on the bench is, "I don't want to make any more mistakes." This leads to the player, often the whole team, playing in a tentative manner. They are scared to make mistakes, so they focus only on not making any mistakes, not on what they should be doing on the court. The players take few chances, do not play aggressively, and are often much slower because they are thinking, instead of playing. You can tell when teams play in a tentative manner like this. If a player makes a mistake and instantly looks at the coach, there is a problem because he or she fears the coach is going to pull him or her out soon. This was the story of Fred's team; many of the players were tentative and would look over to the coach when they made a mistake. By substituting often, the coach reinforced tentative play in his players.

Also, the coach would put on a show regarding the referees—he was overly dramatic. I know there is an aspect to working the referees, but I felt like Fred's coach went much further than necessary. It seemed to me, if it looked like the team would lose, the coach would want everyone to think, "It's the ref's fault, not mine." By being so dramatic with the referees, the coach acted like this absolved him of all blame for the loss.

In our next session I asked Fred, "Who is number twelve?" I noticed this kid in warm-up; he seemed like an incredible athlete, yet he never played. Fred said, "Oh, he's the best athlete in the school; he's out for the season now, he just plays basketball for fun. He's already signed a scholarship to play baseball in college." Then Fred asked, "Why do you ask? How did you notice him? He never plays." I told Fred that as a former coach I try to see if I can spot the most talented players. I thought this guy was the only one on the court who was as talented as Fred was. Fred was flattered and surprised, but I felt like it was true. It looked to me like Fred had more talent than any of the starters; he liked to hear I thought he was in the same category as number twelve.

Each week Fred would come in and we would go over his games in detail. We went over all aspects of his game and he was now able to see when things were working and when things were not working. He could now correct problems as they arose. Fred's initial progress had been great but lately it was back to the same old grind. He was playing better, but still having some tough times. Then he got a lucky break—Beavis got sick so Fred got to start.

They often played two games in a week, so when I saw Fred we went over both games. In the first game, when he started, he had a solid game, scored sixteen points, had eight assists and held his opponent to eight points. The guy he was guarding was the other team's top scorer and averaged about seventeen points a game. In the next game, of course, Beavis started; he made a quick comeback from being sick, the scrappy little guy he was.

How did this all end? Fred's team made the playoffs. For their first playoff game Fred played about half the game, primarily during the second half, and still scored fourteen points.

By this time I had introduced myself to his parents, though I did not sit with them at games. Actually, they did not even sit together because watching the game was too intense of an experience for them to do together. Both his mom and dad were pleased with Fred's progress. Scoring fourteen points, Fred was the second highest scorer on the team. Beavis scored two points that game, his season average, but he did look good diving for loose balls.

During the next playoff game, Fred's team was down by ten points in the first quarter. When Fred finally got in the game he hit three three-point shots in a row and helped his team get back into the game. When the coach pulled Fred out, I wanted to scream. With Fred in the game the momentum quickly shifted to his team. His team was now down by three points and Fred was back on the bench. I could not believe that what was obvious to me, and those sitting around me, was not obvious to the coach. The coach would live and die with Beavis.

Late in the game Fred got back in and stayed in (Beavis twisted his ankle). At this point his team was again down by ten points. It was as if nothing had changed since the start of the season with the coach—he wanted to see if Fred was hot. Fred hit three two-point shots and two free throws. He now had seventeen points and once again helped make the game close. The star of Fred's team had eighteen points; however, he played twice as many minutes as Fred. Toward the end of the game Fred hit another three-point shot. After a quick turnover by the other team, Fred was fouled while shooting, but missed his two free throws. He finished the game with twenty-two points and was the leading scorer of the game. Had Fred made those two free throws his team may have won the game.

So it ended. Fred played much better, not perfect; he had his ups and downs during the season. For the season Fred was the second leading scorer on the team and was also second in the league in three-point scoring. He did all this while playing about half the amount of time as the starters. I like to think that at one point after the season was over, the coach reflected on these statistics and thought, "I should have played Fred more." However, I am sure that the coach sat in his office and thought, "Wow, that Beavis was a great player."

About four months after the season I got a call from Fred's dad. I was worried something might be going on with Fred. His dad said, "Oh, Fred is fine. He'll be playing at a junior college next year. Actually I'm calling you about my golf game—can you help me?"

CHAPTER 8
Terri—A Depressed Olympian

T he topic of athletes and depression has been publicized a
lot lately. In the past, many people thought athletes should
be immune to depression, or if an athlete experienced depression he or she was seen as weak and needed to snap out of
it. Depression is an incredibly complex subject. My views about
depression and its treatment may appear a little different from
many mental health professionals.

Terri came to see me during the Spring break of her sophomore year of college. Terri is a water polo player who grew up
here in the San Francisco Bay Area, but went out of the area to
attend college. In high school, Terri had been very successful,
named U.S. Player of the Year both her junior and senior years
of high school.

Her college coach, whom I knew from my coaching days,
referred Terri to me. Terri phoned me and told me she would
be coming back to the Bay Area for Spring break and asked if
we could meet as much as possible while she was back in town.
Terri's Spring break was two weeks before she was to compete
in the NCAA Water Polo Championships. Her coaches, friends,
and parents were concerned about her.

When Terri came in to see me she gave me a brief history.
She told me that after her senior year she was invited to try
out for the U.S. National team. The National team consists of
both an "A" and "B" team. Terri was selected for the "B" team.
Quickly, she impressed the coaches so much she was promoted

to the "A" Team. As a member of the "A" team she was selected to be part of the U.S. Olympic team. She was the only
college freshman on the U.S. team and was many years younger
than her teammates.

Although the San Francisco Bay Area is a large metropoli-
tan area, it is made up of smaller communities; many have their
own local newspapers. Being named to the U.S. Olympic team,
Terri got quite a bit of notoriety. Her picture was in her local
paper, complete with a lengthy article. Her friends and water
polo team members threw her a big party when the U.S. Olympic Water Polo Team was announced. It seemed to Terri that
everyone in her town knew about her success.

Terri expected to get some playing time at the Olympics and
hoped to provide a positive impact on the team.

Terri reported to me that while preparing for and competing in the Olympic Games, she was in awe of her teammates.
She was now on the same national team as many of the water
polo players she had read about for years. Terri said she had a
feeling of unreality about the whole experience. Since many of
the girls on the Olympic Team were much older, Terri kept to
herself most of the time up to and during the Olympics. Looking back she realized she was very lonely and isolated during the
whole experience.

The Water Polo competition at the Olympic Games was
over a six-day period. Terri was incredibly nervous about playing in the Olympic Games. In the first couple rounds of play,
typically the U.S. team has an easy time with their competition.
Terri was so overwhelmed by the Olympic experience that she
felt more like a spectator than a competitor.

Terri played in the first two games, which the U.S. team easily won. She felt like she did not play well at all. She said, "I
made some bad passes, turned the ball over way too much, I
often missed my defensive assignment and allowed my defender

to score too much." She did not play in the last two rounds of the Olympics. The U.S. team won a Bronze Medal. After the Olympics Terri was demoted back to the "B" team.

When Terri came home from the trip, she decided to take a little time off from water polo. Terri said she felt like she was burnt out.

When Terri started her freshman year of college, she began to realize all the things she had missed over the years because of her commitment to water polo. Terri, like most national caliber water polo players, would wake up around 5:00 A.M., go to polo practice for two hours, then to school and practice another two hours after school. Terri had kept up this rigorous schedule since ninth grade. She began to resent water polo and all it had taken from her, namely a social life. Athletes dream of making it to the top. However, after they have competed at the highest level in sports, they often feel let down. Terri experienced a severe let-down after the Olympic Games.

Terri told me that during her freshman year of college, "My heart wasn't into water polo at all. I just went through the motions." Terri said that she began to use food as a way to comfort herself from feeling overwhelmed. She felt like she was trapped. She did not want to quit water polo because she felt she needed to honor her commitment to her college team. However, she wanted a social life and, especially, she wanted to date. She had not dated much at all during high school. Terri said she was not part of the popular crowd in high school and was very lonely. In college she felt overwhelmed, being away from home, family, and friends. As she began her freshman year of college, she realized nothing was likely to change. She dreaded another year of polo practice, tournaments, and more practice. She began to wonder, "What's the point of making water polo my whole life?"

As her freshman year dragged on, Terri gained about ten pounds by Christmas. Her parents were concerned that Terri was isolating from others and that she did not seem very happy. During Christmas break, they took Terri to a psychiatrist, who prescribed Terri an antidepressant. Two months later, Terri or her parents did not see any change at all in Terri's mood, so the psychiatrist upped the dosage of the antidepressant. Over the following summer, the psychiatrist once again upped the dosage.

One of the side effects of antidepressants can be weight gain; by the time I saw Terri she had put on about twenty pounds since the Olympic Games. There is a crude saying in the sport of swimming that "fat girls don't swim fast." How fast a water polo player can swim really affects his or her ability to succeed in water polo. In Terri's position in water polo, her speed in the water was an important factor. Terri felt much more depressed when I saw her than she did when she started taking the antidepressants. She felt like she was not near the water polo player she was just two years before. In high school, Terri had been the dominant player; in college she was just an average player. Prior to starting college, Terri was expected to be a college star; her team was counting on her to lead them to the NCAA Championships. Now, Terri looked like a polo player who had reached her peak in high school and was on her way down.

Terri told me she felt so bad earlier in the school year that she thought about staying home over Christmas break and not returning to college. She dreaded playing in the NCAA Championships in two weeks because she knew she would not perform at the level she used to. Terri felt embarrassed with herself and with the way she was playing now. Tearfully, she said, "I feel like I have let everyone down."

Terri's parents were going to make the trip across the country to watch her compete in the NCAA Championships; they had made their reservations months ago. Her parents were supportive, not pushy, and Terri described them as "my best friends." Yet

Terri still did not know how to talk with them, or anyone, about what had happened in her life in the past two years.

At the end of our first session I said, "I want you to know there is a way out of this mess, and you can get back to playing like you used to." I told Terri that the process back to her pre-Olympic performance level would take some time and for right now she had to get through the last two weeks of this season.

I recommended to Terri that she get off antidepressants completely. She said, "That's interesting, I talked with the psychiatrist yesterday and he wanted to up the dosage again." I suggested to Terri that she read the book *Prozac Backlash*, by Joseph Glenmullen, MD. Glenmullen is a psychiatrist at Harvard who stated that many people are unnecessarily on antidepressants. Glenmullen points out that the effectiveness of antidepressants on teenagers is not clear at all. Terri was nineteen years old when I saw her.

There is a difference between being depressed and having a depressive disorder. Terri was depressed; she did not have a depressive disorder. I knew that if Terri lost weight and was playing much better she would not be depressed anymore and would not need antidepressants. The antidepressants were dealing with the symptoms of Terri's depression, not the cause of her depression. The cause of her depression was that Terri was lonely, had very low self-esteem, and was incredibly hard on herself. She had a very hard time asserting herself with anyone and had no social support other than her parents. She was ashamed of her weight gain and embarrassed by her play lately. She had a hard time adjusting to college and being away from home. She felt inferior to everyone.

As we talked, Terri realized that the antidepressants had not helped her at all, even when the dosage was increased. Terri said, "In fact, when I think about it, I'm more depressed now than when I started taking the antidepressants." I pointed out to Terri that if we were sitting here one year from now and she was poised to play great in the NCAA Tournament, she would not be depressed. I told her we needed to focus on the things that would make her feel better about herself. The answer was not in a pill.

The problem at hand was how to get through the upcoming NCAA Championships. In college water polo, the NCAA Championships are the sole focus of the top teams in the country. Terri, being an Olympian, was expected to do well in the Championships. However, from her poor performance the last two seasons along with her weight gain, both of us knew there was no way she

There is a difference between being depressed and having a depressive disorder. Terri was depressed; she did not have a depressive disorder. I knew that if Terri lost weight and was playing much better she would not be depressed anymore and would not need antidepressants. The antidepressants were dealing with the symptoms of Terri's depression, not the cause of her depression.

was ready to perform well. Terri was scared she would embarrass herself, her coach, her parents, and her team at NCAAs. Terri said she felt "listless and heavy in the water." She said she would rather not compete in the NCAAs at all; however, that was not an option for her.

Terri did say she was feeling better that she was finally able to talk about all the things that had been bothering her for some time. The more we talked the less daunting the NCAAs seemed. Many times simply talking about their problems helps athletes release much of the pressure that they feel.

I suggested to Terri that she use this year's NCAAs as a dress rehearsal for the next two years. I pointed out that although she, her coach, and her teammates may be disappointed, next year could be a different story. We also talked about how she could try to do the best she could under the circumstances. We adjusted her expectations to trying to play her best games of the season, not the best games of her life.

Terri told me she really wished her parents were not going to the NCAAs. She said although she knows they support and love her, she would rather they not see her play poorly. Terri said that she had been on the phone crying often to her parents during the past few months. Her parents were at a loss at what to do and were glad her coach suggested that Terri meet with me. When I called her father to discuss billing, he told me, "I'm just glad she has someone to talk to."

Before Terri left we came up with a plan for her to taper off the antidepressants. As Glenmullen points out in *Prozac Backlash*, many people have withdrawal symptoms when coming off antidepressants. We agreed not to change anything until after the NCAA Championships. Terri went back to school and we agreed to meet when she returned to the Bay Area for the summer.

I checked the NCAA results online and saw Terri's team got third place at the NCAAs. Terri did score a couple goals in the tournament, but was not named to the All Tournament team.

When Terri returned for the summer we were able to meet on a consistent basis. She was back playing with her former team and had a great relationship with her local coach. After the NCAA Tournament, Terri gradually cut down her antidepressants and was now completely off medication.

We began to look at Terri's relationship with food. She admitted that over the past two years she used food to comfort herself. She ate when she was bored or lonely. Terri had run cross-country her freshman year in high school and now began running a couple times a week. She began to try to stop and notice how she was feeling before she started to eat. Terri tried to eat only when she was hungry and started to eat healthier meals. College food has a lot of starch and many girls put on weight.

As our sessions progressed we began to explore some of Terri's deeper issues. She said, "Looking back on high school, I only had a few friends." Even with her success in water polo in high school, Terri's self-esteem was terrible. Since starting college and gaining weight, her self-esteem dropped even lower. When I asked about her self-esteem now, she told me that her self-esteem was at the lowest point she could ever remember.

I asked Terri why her self-esteem was so low. Terri told me she was not comfortable with her body at all. She said she wished that she were prettier and thinner. She said that she compares herself to other girls and feels she does not measure up. She said that when she goes out with her teammates in college she ends up taking care of anyone who gets too drunk. She said she feels like she is a better friend to others than they are to her. Terri told me that she often agrees to do something with others rather than assert herself and say what she really wants to do. She feels that if she stands up to anyone, they will not want to be her friend. She does not feel she has anything to offer anyone.

When Terri told me, "I don't like myself at all." I said, "Tell me what you don't like about yourself." Terri said, "I think I'm fat, I'm not pretty enough and I think my hair is ugly." Terri's evaluation of herself was externally based. Next, I said to Terri, "Now that you have told me what you do not like about yourself, tell me what you do like about yourself." Terri got quiet, thought for a while, a tear welled up in her eye, and then she looked me in the eye and said, "Nothing, there is nothing at all that I like about myself." I said, "Wait a second here, you're nice, friendly, honest, hard working, have a good sense of humor, you're loyal and a good friend to others." She halfway nodded in agreement. I said, "How is it that I see these things in you after only meeting with you a few times, yet you can not see these things within yourself?" Terri was speechless.

I explained to Terri something I have heard Thich Nhat Hanh, author of the book *Living Buddha, Living Christ*, say. Hanh said that if we go to a dumpsite we would obviously see a lot of garbage. Growing out of the garbage we would see flowers. He points out that this is how all of us are internally. We all have our own garbage and our own flowers inside of us. Hanh asks if we only see our own garbage, or do we see our flowers too? Do we, he asked, only see garbage in others? He points out that we should focus on the flowers within ourselves as well as the flowers in others. Terri saw her garbage. I saw her flowers. I asked her to focus more on her flowers and ignore her garbage.

Contrary to Hanh, I told Terri that I wanted her to look for garbage in others too. She seemed to hold girls she thought were pretty on a pedestal. I told her that everyone has issues and I wanted her to look for some of their garbage. I wanted Terri to see that the people she wanted to be like had their own garbage too. At the same time I told her that she was to focus on her own flowers and the flowers of those close to her. By noticing and nurturing her flowers, it would be easier to deal with her garbage.

Terri began to lose weight and get in better shape; her water polo play began to improve. As we talked about the upcoming Summer National Championships Terri began to express some of her fears. She said, "I don't know if I want to put it all on the line again, just to fail." She talked about how hard she worked out before the Olympic Games and how crushed she was that she did not play well. I told her that I hardly saw her Olympic experience as a failure. Sure, she did not play her best, but she was playing with and against the best players in the world. Even if she had played her best, she still may not have played much more in the Olympics as many of her teammates had been on the national team for years. I pointed out that there were many possible explanations for her play, other than not having what it takes to succeed at the highest level of her sport.

One of the things we had been working on changing was how hard Terri was on herself. She told me that in the past she knew she was never satisfied with her performance. The same drive that pushed her daily in practice and in competition produced thoughts after a tournament that she could have played better. She said, "Why should I even bother trying to make the Olympic team again, because I know I will be upset with myself for winning only one Gold Medal." Terri had put herself in a no-win situation. If she played great it was not good enough; if she did not she was a failure.

I talked with Terri about the difference between being afraid to try and being afraid to succeed. Terri's fear of putting it all on the line again really took away the possibility of her having to face the pain and frustration of failing. She would not have the opportunity to fail at an international tournament if she did not put it all on the line again. I told Terri that for her to succeed she had to commit to not just going through the motions, as she had been doing the past two years. We needed to shift her focus to what she was doing in practice each day. I suggested she try to put it all on the line in practice each day.

I also recommended to Terri that I did not think it was a good idea for her to continue to plan her outcomes. Terri knew before the tournament how she expected to play, she already had the result pre-programmed in her head, and if she failed to live up to her incredibly high standards, she saw herself as a failure. Planning her outcomes in the past led to pain and frustration. Even when she competed in the Olympics she was not happy, because the outcome she planned included playing much better than she did and winning a Gold Medal. Although she made the Olympic Team, it was not quite good enough in her mind. I told Terri, "You need to give yourself a break." I pointed out that she was way more critical of herself than all the other people in her life combined. By not planning her outcomes, she could play her hardest and accept whatever result followed. I asked her to quit judging herself.

As we continued to meet, Terri told me she was noticing a difference in herself since she had quit taking the antidepressants. Terri said, "I feel much more responsive and active now. When I was on the medication, I felt like a zombie and constantly in a trance." Terri reported her parents commented that she seemed to be back to her old self again.

Terri had now lost much of the weight she had gained and her water polo play really started to pick up. Much of water polo practice is swimming. Terri said that the day before, she swam great. She said she crushed everyone on her team during a swimming set, including many other national caliber players. Her coach told her after the practice that it was the best practice he had seen her swim in years and probably one of the best practices he had ever seen her swim. The coach commented on both Terri's speed in the water and her ball handling skills. He told Terri she was playing water polo like an Olympian again. Terri's self-confidence was growing.

Terri began asserting herself more too. The previous weekend some of the girls on her team called Terri and asked if she wanted to go party in the city with them. Terri did not want to go; in the past she would have gone, had a bad time, ended up taking care of one or more of the girls, then beaten herself up emotionally afterward. This time she told them, "I'm just gonna hang out around here and take it easy tonight." She ended up going to a movie with one of her other friends, and had a nice time.

As the summer National Championships approached, Terri was feeling ready to play great. We went over Terri's past successful tournaments and reviewed how she would approach her games. The progress Terri made over the summer was obvious to everyone. She was once again excited about water polo and was much more accepting of herself. She was no longer depressed. Antidepressants do not deal with why someone is depressed. Terri clearly had been depressed for specific reasons. Now, her self-esteem had improved and she was asserting herself much more; she had lost weight and was playing much better. She had created a better emotional support system. By talking in therapy about things Terri had kept inside her for a long time, she was able to resolve many of the emotional issues that had plagued her for two years. The reasons for Terri's depression were now gone. Thus, her depression was gone.

After the National Championships Terri was going on vacation with her family, then returning to college. Terri played great at the National Championships and was named to the All Tournament Team. The U.S. National coach told Terri she was impressed with Terri's level of play. She told Terri she was moving Terri back up to the "A" National Team and said she would like to have Terri represent the U.S. in the World University Games a few months away. The coach praised Terri on how she played, looked, and conducted herself in the tournament.

Terri ended up competing all four years of college. She was also on the U.S. National team for the next four years and ended up playing once again in the Olympics, played great, and won a Bronze Medal. With self-confidence and a belief that she could get through the setbacks, she was able to retire satisfied with her career. Terri could have easily ended up a broken egg.

CHAPTER 9

Guidelines for Coaches

Teach

In my view every good coach is a good teacher. You should
not just tell athletes what you want them to do. Teach them
how to do it. I am surprised at how many children do not
know how to throw a ball properly. The first step of any Little
League coach should be teaching the kids the proper mechanics
of throwing and catching a ball. Every skill a young child needs
to learn should be taught over and over.

As a coach I thought that swimmers swam by habit, so most
of the work I did to try to change their strokes came in the form
of stroke drills. I would have them do drills that made them
swim with proper technique. I knew if I just told them what to
do, they would do it for a few minutes, then go back to their old
habits. Changing habits takes time. Every athlete I ever coached
did stroke drills every single day. You should not just teach a
skill one day and then move on. Incorporate drills daily into
your practice that force kids to have the proper technique.

Teaching also means educating the players about the position they are playing. This should include a job description. By
this I mean that the coach should have written out everything he
or she expects from someone playing that position. An example in basketball would be the point guard position. The coach
should have a list of everything he or she expects the point
guard to do. Often the coach just tells the point guard, "I want
you to be the leader on the court." The instruction needs to

152

be much more specific, like, "The point guard calls and directs plays. It is the point guard's responsibility to tell other players if they are out of position." Many young children are reluctant to play point guard because they do not understand all of the responsibilities that come with playing the position.

In the work world most people have a job description. Their performance in tangible areas of their job is evaluated. It would help athletes if they had the same type of guidelines. Often coaches expect players to know every nuance of their position. These nuances need to be defined and then taught. There is an inherent problem with this approach. The higher you go in sports the more coaches are judged by their win/loss record. Because of this they often only emphasize winning and losing. They get caught up in the wins and losses and do not spend enough time teaching. If they win a game, they move to the next game and do not use the win as a teaching opportunity. It is important to be constantly teaching and learning regardless of whether things go right or go wrong. Learn from both your successes and failures.

When correcting technique, you should explain and show your athletes what they are doing, what you want them to do, and what they need to do to make the necessary changes. Too many coaches simply say things like "you're off balance, follow through more, keep your elbows up, you're swinging too fast." A coach should explain step by step how to make the changes he or she wants an athlete to make.

Make Practice Interesting and Interactive

It seems every Little League practice I see is the same. The players are out in the field and the coach hits balls to them. Let's look at the outfielder: typically in Little League these are the less skilled players. They need to work on catching fly balls. Let's say that while in the outfield the coach hits a person five balls, which is much more than usual, as the coach is hitting balls to everyone. Of those five balls, two or three will be uncatchable. They are hit far enough away from the kids that they cannot get to them in time to catch the ball. During the course of practice, the outfielder may get two balls hit to him or her that are catchable balls. My suggestion is to pair the kids up and have them throw balls to each other. They can throw fly balls, grounders, bouncers, whatever. Pairing the kids up means they will each get many more catchable balls. By having the kids work in pairs they can vary distances and will have many more attempts at practicing how to catch a ball properly.

This catching drill could come first. Then the kids can work on catching the ball out in the field, because I am well aware that the ball comes off a bat differently when hit than when thrown. However, if the kid can't catch the ball no matter what, then what difference does it make? When I see a Little League coach hitting the balls to kids, I think it is more for the coach's ego than the kid's benefit. Kids could start by slowly rolling the ball to each other to learn the proper technique for fielding a grounder. The coach could instruct each player because in the long run, learning and practicing the basics is essential.

Michael Sokolove, in his book *The Ticket Out: Darryl Strawberry and the Boys of Crenshaw*, talks about the use of stations during practice. The Crenshaw High School baseball team of 1979 is arguably the greatest high school baseball team ever. Brooks Hurst, Crenshaw's coach, incorporated stations into practice. Each station worked on a specific skill, and the players rotated from station to station during practice. With the use of stations, Coach Hurst was able to make practice interesting and interactive for the players, preventing boredom.

Also, many coaches have the mistaken belief that a practice has to be serious. Remember that a practice can still be challenging and fun, yet intense. Try to avoid monotony in your practices. One of the best ways to do this is to come up with games or competitions during practice that are challenging but fun. If you coach a high school sport where running is part of practice, do relays, or have the kids bring a CD player and let them play music while they run. If it is a sport with a ball, you could have them run with a teammate and pass the ball back and forth. If you find a way to make a game out of challenging tasks, you will be surprised at how much extra energy your athletes have.

Work With Your Weaker Players

This is a problem at almost all levels of sport. The coaches often just play the talented kids in games. In practice most of the coach's time is devoted to the best players. In any team sport the depth of talent on your team is key. With kids, the good ones are going to get better almost on their own, but if you help improve the skill level of your second-tier kids, your team will be much more successful. Take basketball for example; the starting five will improve all season. The key to the success of the team is getting the number six through twelve players to improve. There will come a time when the game comes down to these second-tier players. Since they are not as good as the starters at the beginning of the season, they often can make progress in leaps and bounds. Coaches frequently do not give these kids enough attention because it is a lot of work for the coaches to actually coach them. Structure your practices so these kids have plenty of time to work on their skills. Transform these players from bystanders to integral members of the team.

With kids, the good ones are going to get better almost on their own, but if you help improve the skill level of your second-tier kids, your team will be much more successful.

Always Try to Gain Knowledge

Confucius once stated that the essence of knowledge is having it to use. If you don't have the knowledge to coach—

work to get it. In the day of the Internet there is no reason not to have the knowledge you need to teach the necessary skills in your sport. No matter what level of coaching you are doing, you should always look at new ideas. There are coaches that have the same approach every single season. If they coach for twenty years, they have coached one year, twenty times. They have not changed anything or gained any knowledge. I remember that after I finished my first season coaching at Cal. I felt I knew everything. I soon realized how little I actually knew. Coaching is like life—the more you learn, the more unanswered questions you have.

Don't Be Too Rigid

One problem I see for kids is that they hear the same thing from every coach from the time they are eight years old. Each coach says the kids need to be committed to the sport. The coach wants them to put all their energy into their sport. This approach is detrimental to the development of young athletes. Trying to force kids to commit at an early age is one thing that causes them to quit when they reach high school. By the time these kids get to high school they want some free time for themselves. If you are coaching anyone under the age of twelve, you should allow, and encourage, them to do more than one sport. If you are a high school coach, look at what is in the athlete's best interest, not yours.

In swimming most kids swim for professional swim coaches on club teams. These are called U.S. Swimming teams, the old AAU. Coaching swimming is what these people do for a living and they are often well qualified. The high school coach, more often than not, is someone who has another career and coaches high school for fun. They may think they know a lot, but they are nowhere near as qualified as the professional coach. If you are coaching high school swimming, and the athletes are working with a professional coach, do not demand that these kids practice with the high school team. Let them swim with their club coach and show up only for the high school swim meets. They do not need to be committed to the high school swim team. In reality, they could teach the coach and other athletes about commitment, as these are athletes who are getting up at 5:00 A.M. or earlier to go to their U.S. Swimming practice before school.

The same holds true for sports like golf and tennis. I see too many high school coaches that expect commitment from the athletes, yet they are not competent to coach the sport at a high level. Because these coaches wear so many hats in life they are not able to give their athletes the same quality of coaching that a professional coach provides. This is a sad and tragic situation for these young athletes. Athletes often get more recognition at school for being on their school team than they do for working with their professional coach. There is also pressure from their peers to be on the high school team. The problem is that their overall performance suffers when they compete for nonprofessional coaches.

Good Sportsmanship is Key

No matter how good the athlete is, do not tolerate poor sportsmanship. Many kids who have tantrums do so because they are very insecure. The tantrum is a way to show that "I am a better player than this." If kids cannot control their behavior, take them out of the game or make them do something extra. I think they should do some extra running or experience some form of mild punishment if their behavior is out of line.

As a coach, you should act the way you want your athletes to act. Let them know that it is your job to talk to the referee, not theirs. When you talk to a referee, do so with respect. You can argue the call, but don't berate the person. Also, if the referee or umpire is an older kid, give him or her a break. If the umpire for your Little League game is sixteen, perhaps talk to him alone after, not during, the game. Also, do not allow the parents of your kids to berate the umpire or referee.

Praise Often

You should focus on what your kids are doing right. Too often the parent and the coach focus on what the kid is doing wrong. You should praise kids in front of everyone and criticize in private. Too frequently I see the coaches belittling kids in front of the rest of the team. This is a crime and can cause long-lasting emotional damage for kids. For young kids, there is not much worse than being embarrassed in front of your peers. The only time this is necessary is if the child's behavior is totally out of line. A mistake in how a child is playing is not a reason to embarrass the child in front of his or her peers. You should strive to find something good to say about each kid daily.

When you do need to talk with an athlete, do so in private. It is best to wait at least one day for both of you to calm down. Then the two of you can sit down, in private, and try to talk things out. Only if talking one on one does not work do you include the child's parents. You should not let other kids on the team know the results of your talk, or when the time comes for you to talk with them, they will not open up.

I am reminded here of Karen Moe Thornton, the women's swim coach at Cal when I worked with the men's team. Karen is a former World Record holder and Olympic Gold Medalist. Karen swam for Santa Clara Swim Club in the 1970s. Karen said her coach, George Haines, tried to make each person on the team feel like they were his favorite. Make each of the kids you coach feel like he or she is your favorite.

Don't Use Your Kids for Your Benefit

Too many coaches try to live out their coaching or playing fantasies when coaching children. Keep in mind you are there for their best interest—not the other way around. Do not emulate the professional coaches you see on television, especially the ones that act inappropriately. Always remember you are dealing with children. Any survey ever done on kids in sports lists "having fun" as a child's number one goal in playing a sport. Make it your goal as a coach. I think the definition of fun changes over time. For young kids fun is going out for pizza or ice cream after the game. Improving as a player is a lot of fun too. When you get older winning is fun. Unfortunately, now there is too much pressure to win too soon in these young athletes' careers. If, as a coach, you are clear about what is for your benefit and what is best for the kids, everyone's experience is much better.

> Make each of the kids you coach feel like he or she is your favorite.

I remember once I was asked to speak to a group of Little League coaches. Someone had heard me speak to a parent group about good sportsmanship and the need to nurture young athletes and asked if I would talk at their Little League meeting. When I started talking about the need to not pressure the kids too much, all the coaches seemed in agreement and did not understand why I was even there talking to them. They felt like they knew all this stuff. When I opened things up for discussion, one coach talked about being banned from All Star games because as the third base coach, he was heckling the opposing pitcher. The coach said, "I knew I could get into the pitcher's head, and if I did, we could win."

The coaches also talked about how important it was to them to try to win each game. They had a rivalry with each other and each wanted to outdo the other. It seemed their self-worth was tied into how their team did and it was as if they felt like if they won they would get recognized as a coach and move on to bigger and better things. The kids they coached were about ten years old.

Ban All Star Teams for Kids Under the Age of Twelve

As a coach, do what you can to ban All Star teams. Every coach wants to coach the All Star team because it makes him or her look great. However, being left off the All Star team has a big impact on how the kid sees him- or herself. Sports for kids under the age of twelve should just be a fun time where they learn a lot. All Star teams do not help younger kids at all. Let's look at the impact they have on the kids not making the All Star team. They feel they do not measure up, they get discouraged, and then may be reluctant to keep playing the sport. This is especially true if year after year they are left off the All Star team. A tall lanky kid may have the potential to be a great athlete, but at a young age, he or she is awkward and probably will not be All Star material.

For those that make the All Star team, it trains them to be results oriented rather than process oriented. By results oriented, I mean making the All Star team, rather than the process of improving, becomes the season's goal. The process of improving is what will lead to long-term success in a sport. There will be a time when all the kids move up to the next level. Most of the kids will then be at the bottom of the ladder. If they are process oriented they can work to improve their skills. If they are results oriented all they see is they aren't as good as everyone else and quitting seems reasonable. After all, they can not make the All Star team, so why bother to play anyway. Making the All Star team, at a young age, does not teach them the need for the hard work they will need to do when they are at the bottom of the ladder.

When I am talking about an All Star team here, I am referring to Select teams. These are separate teams during the season. Select teams are more like their own All Star League. I think it is fine for ten- to twelve-year-olds to go to one competition at the end of the season, like one game or one swim meet. However, before the age of twelve, they do not need to be in Championship Tournaments or on travel teams.

If you feel my approach of banning All Star teams for twelve-and-unders is too radical, then ban them for ten-and-unders. If you think eight and unders should have All Star teams, you really should rethink why you are coaching. And if you think six and unders should be on All Star teams, you should never attend any of your kids' games because you will pressure them way too much. They will quit sports and resent you pushing them.

The best kids under the age of twelve are the most coordinated ones and the ones that develop the fastest. In swimming the age groups are split up into ten-and-unders, then elevens and twelves. Once, I had a kid on my team who had turned eleven the week before the swim meet, so he was eleven years and one week old, swimming in the eleven and twelve age group. He had to swim against kids that were going to turn thirteen the next weekend. I saw my young swimmer crying before it was time to race and I asked him what was wrong. He replied, "I'm not swimming against a kid with a mustache." One kid that was just about to turn thirteen had a mustache, he was a fast swimmer because he hit puberty early and was bigger and stronger, and of course, he was on the All Star team. It was the highlight of his career, which soon ended.

When we look at burn-out, it often comes after years and years of pressure to win championships and to make All Star teams. By making sports fun for the younger kids, the chances are that they will stay in sports longer. Only when the kids are twelve or older do I feel they are ready to be on All Star teams.

Keep the Parents of Your Kids in Line

Do not let the parents of the kids you coach yell at the referees, players, coaches, or even their own children. Support rules in your league to have disruptive parents removed or even banned from games. Even if you agree that the referee made a mistake, you should do the talking, not the parents.

Remember how self-conscious these young kids are. I have had many kids come to see me because some parent yelled at them; sometimes these are the parents of their own teammates. One twelve-year-old catcher dropped the ball and allowed the winning run to score. The boy said one parent yelled from the stands, "Way to go Jimmy, you cost us the game." When he was leaving he overheard two other parents saying, "I don't know why the coach had Jimmy playing catcher anyway. He always drops the ball." This kid said to me, "Why should I play? I want to have fun. I hate getting yelled at; since I'm the catcher, I hear everything they say in the stands." This affected not only his baseball performance, but also his overall self-confidence as a person. These parents did not seem to realize, or care, that he was a twelve-year-old child. They cared more about winning than the kids on the team did.

Do Not Transmit Pressure

Often coaches at the high school level and above are under a lot of pressure because more and more schools want their coaches to deliver victories. The coach is under tremendous pressure to keep winning so he or she can keep his or her job. The key here is not to transmit this pressure onto your team, because athletes can feel when you are really stressed out. Be careful not to conduct yourself in a way that says, "We have got to win." The athletes translate this into you saying—"We have to win or I am out of a job." This is when athletes often feel that the coach is freaking out.

How do you keep from transmitting the pressure you feel onto your team? You should have your own outlet for dealing with your pressures. You should have friends, family members, or other coaches you can use for support. Do not bring up your

issue of feeling like you have to win with the team. It will only cause more problems.

Share Snack Time

In many sports' leagues, like Little League, parents bring a snack for the kids after each game. If you coach in a league that has a snack after the game, I suggest your team and the other team share the snack together. This helps build good sportsmanship and camaraderie. It is important for young kids not to see the opposing team as the enemy. Even high school teams could get together once in a while for a picnic after a game. I know this sounds strange, but if you try it, you will be surprised at how good it turns out.

Goal Setting

I think the saying, "There is no 'I' in team" has been over-used. I am going to suggest something that may seem radical: rethink your team goals—or even the concept of focusing on having team goals.

If kids commit to how THEY are going to run, swim, shoot, or throw, they are taking ownership of their goals. I think team goals are nebulous. Winning the game or the championship lacks personal responsibility.

There is an "I" in Improve. Athletes should focus on their own improvement. Thus, I think goals primarily should be individual. Each person on the team should know what he or she wants to, and is willing to commit to, improve on. Team goals are often "win the championship," or "make the playoffs." I would rather each person commit specifically to what he or she wants to contribute to the team. "I want to have my free throw percentage at 85%" is a specific goal that person can commit to work toward. If kids commit to how **THEY** are going to run, swim, shoot, or throw, they are taking ownership of their goals. I think team goals are nebulous. Winning the game or the championship lacks personal responsibility.

Often coaches put 90% of their effort in focusing on what they want to have happen, like win it all, and 10% of their energy into how they want to accomplish this goal. They have it backwards; 10% of your effort should be where you want to go—to the championship—and 90% should be about what specifically you will do to get there.

Too often coaches have the team's goal in mind before the season starts or they even know who is on their team, "We're here to win, right?" You have to make each person responsible for his or her own improvement for the team goals to fall into place. In other words, if each member of the basketball team commits to how he or she can improve, the team has a much better chance of winning the championship.

If the number eight through twelve players rarely play, how do they fit into the team's goals? What is the area in which they are going to improve? It is much easier for them to go along for the ride with the team goal. Then at the end of the season, when one starter has fouled out, one person is sick, another is out for grades, all of a sudden the seventh through the twelfth players become very important. This is why earlier I wrote about the importance of working with the weaker players. If all season long the "B" players have stuck to their own goals and worked on them, then they can help the team when they are needed most. If they are getting into important games late in the season and have not worked on their own goals, there probably will be problems. When they fail, it is usually interpreted as "They choked and can't handle pressure." I see this as the coaches' fault for not preparing the players properly.

By having their own goals, players are accountable during the season. They have worked daily in practice on things they needed to work on. Think of the difference in confidence for these players further down the bench. If they have been improving all season long, they will be much more confident during high-pressure situations. Their confidence will not be near as good if they have just been swept along with the team goal.

Also when a team's goal is to win the championship, what happens when they start the season 0-4? These teams often suffer from a lack of direction. They have a kind of dazed "now what?" look on their faces, and the coaches are in the same boat here too. If they have told the team all along that they want to win and halfway through the season it is obvious they cannot win the championship, they are lost. They don't know quite what to do with the team. Do they rehash the goals, or focus on next year? Often if a team loses the first four or five games they will talk about getting above .500. The focus should be on individual improvement, not the outcome.

Having individual goals also comes into play if any of the key players gets injured. If the focus has always been the team goal, it can be harder for a player to step up and replace an injured person. Also, if some of the key players get hurt, it is possible some of the other players will have the attitude of "We can't win the championship without our stars." This attitude undermines their commitment and their intensity. Often players in these situations don't believe that the team can win. Had the focus been on each player's individual performance, the situation could have a different outcome.

Even in team sports like football, basketball, soccer, volleyball, and baseball this approach is key. All players need to walk away from the game and evaluate how they did in respect to their own goals. If the team wins, and someone does not play well, it is easier to overlook his or her performance if everything is only focused on the team goal. If the team wins, but a player only shot 60% from the free throw line, perhaps he should work on his free throws more to reach his individual goals.

Most people know goals should be measurable, in order to know you are making progress toward your goals. When the goals are individualized, they are much easier to measure. Furthermore, if a team's goal is to make the playoffs, how does the team refocus once they have reached their goal? By having individual, specific, measurable goals, all players, at any time in the season, should know how they are doing in regard to their goals.

Often problems with team cohesion arise because some players feel they are doing all the work and that other players are just along for the ride. These problems often lead to jealousy and resentment amongst team members. When each person is accountable, it can help with team cohesion.

Here is an example for a high school basketball team. Often coaches have a talk at the beginning of the season that goes something like this: "This season I want you guys to give one hundred and ten percent in practice every day. We are going to out-hustle our opponents. We are going to win the championship this year and I expect all of you to be committed to winning. If you don't want to win—you might as well leave right now. I want to see intensity from you every day. We need to focus and be dedicated to reaching our goal of winning the championship. You have got to have a winning attitude to win the championship."

Here is another option. "Last year we lost six games by less than ten points. We need to improve our overall free throw shooting percentage. In each of those games we could have won had we done better from the free throw line. Each Friday at the end of practice we will each shoot ten free throws. We will keep a running tally of your free throw percentage both in practice and in games. We want all the players on this team to improve their free throw percentage this season. We are going to grade the guards each game on your passing, defense, ball handling, turnovers, and shooting. We want to decrease the number of turnovers for our guards this season. We will look for you each game to try to limit your turnovers. We will look not only at the number of assists you get but your overall passing too. By this we mean seeing the open man and throwing sharp crisp passes. For you low post players, we are looking at rebounding and we will keep stats on offensive and defensive rebounding. We want to see how you are getting in position to get rebounds—how you block out for example. We want to decrease your turnovers as well. Also, for all of you, we will be looking at high percentage shots taken versus low percentage shots taken. We want to see a greater number of high percentage shots taken during the season. Last season we had our low post players taking too many three-point shots. We are looking for the majority of your shots to be close range, high percentage shots. We will do drills each day to work on these specific areas of your game. Each player will be given a goal sheet with specific skills we think you need to work on. There will also be a place on the sheet where you can add any other skills you feel you need to work on. We would like you to fill out the goal sheet and then meet with me to go over your goals and our expectations for you this season. If we want to make it to the Championships this year, this is what we need to do to get us there."

These are two drastically different approaches. Many coaches think by throwing around words like, "intensity," "commitment," "focus," "one hundred and ten percent," "hustle," and "attitude" that they are helping the team reach their goals. Coaches that do this are often not teachers, and remember, every great coach is a great teacher. A great teacher teaches a player how to play the game. The teacher shows how the position should be played and nurtures and helps the player along. A great teacher works with athletes' mistakes, rather than punishes athletes when they make mistakes.

Too many basketball players make a mistake and look over to the coach because they are scared to lose their precious minutes of playing time. They are not learning or improving, they are just trying not to make a mistake that would get them pulled out of the game. A player that does this stagnates and does not improve or get to the next level. They do not try anything new in their game. They just try to stay in the game. They are tentative and there is no flow in their game. Often the coach thinks this is because their opponents intimidate the players, but this is not the case at all. The players are scared of being taken out of the game, sitting on the bench, and not getting their minutes in the future.

Be a Good Counselor

The best coaches are good counselors. Although they may have had little training, many coaches are good counselors. They communicate well with their athletes and are good listeners. My guess is that many of the successful coaches, year in and year out, are great counselors. The more you can relate to your athletes, the more they will see how much you care. Many coaches say they have "an open door policy," but they are not approachable people. Their athletes do not feel comfortable talking to the coach and they feel the coach does not understand them or their problems. One athlete said, "Coach cried when we lost in the playoffs. I don't know if it is because he cared about us or because he wanted to win more for himself." The more you communicate with your athletes, the more they understand you care. Had this coach really cared, the athlete would have known what the tears were about.

Choosing Teams

When dividing up your team for any reason, do not allow the kids to choose the teams—you split them up into teams. When the kids choose, there are always some kids that are picked last. Being picked last is harmful to any kid's self-esteem. Much of their self-esteem is based on what their peers think about them. When you, the coach, split up the teams, you remove this problem. It is quite easy for the coach to split the team up into evenly matched squads. This also saves time, because you can point to the kids and say, "You're a one, you're a two—all the ones over here—all the twos over there." This way no kid is taken last. You should always keep in mind the self-esteem of these fragile young "eggs." Even in high school and college, no one wants to be picked last. Every interaction you have with your athletes should take into consideration their self-esteem.

Respect

Over the years I have heard many coaches say, "You guys need to respect me." Respect is earned, not given. You earn the respect of your players by being a competent coach and by treating your athletes with dignity and respect. You may always have a rude kid or two on your team, but if you feel your whole team does not respect you, take a look at yourself. Great coaches don't need to ask their athletes to respect them, it just happens. I see too many coaches in youth sports trying to demand respect from their athletes. In chemical dependency treatment we say, "If you want to build your self-esteem, you need to do esteem-able deeds." If you want to be respected, act respectful toward your athletes and be a respect-able person.

The Battles Versus the War

At times you will be competing against teams that are much better than your team. The best approach to take in such a situation is to focus on each battle and not worry about who wins the war. Playing against superior teams is one reason I suggest focusing on personal goals rather than team goals.

169

One of my graduate students, Courtney Carroll, was working with a seventeen-year-old girls' soccer team. The team was one of the top teams in their league. The coach thought it would be a good experience for the girls to play a team better than they were. Fortunately, the number one eighteen-year-old girls' team in the country was close by. The coach arranged for a scrimmage between the two teams. It is always a great idea to expose your team to challenging competition.

The first scrimmage between the two teams was Courtney's first week working with the girls. The girls on the team were scared and intimidated by the national champions. Courtney gave them a few suggestions, but the girls were so intimidated about the scrimmage that they didn't really hear what she had to say. The girls lost the scrimmage 9-1. By the end of the game their play was well below what was normal for them. Many of the girls were making excuses for their play or blaming other teammates for the loss.

After the game Courtney and I came up with a plan for the next scrimmage. We decided she should have the girls focus on the battles and not the war. I said, "Go ahead and tell them not to worry about winning the war (game), but they should choose some battles that they can fight." By removing the focus from the outcome of the scrimmage, we were able to get the girls to shift their focus to the fundamentals of the game.

The girls picked four battle areas. First of all, they decided to defend the girl they were guarding much closer by constantly keeping pressure on her. They realized in the first scrimmage they gave the girl they were covering too much room/respect. They decided that they would make the other team work for their goals.

The next battle the girls chose was to really go for 50/50 balls, which are balls both teams have the same chance of getting. In the first scrimmage they were more like 90/10 balls, because Courtney's team figured the girls from the other team would get these loose balls—and they did. Thirdly, the girls decided that no matter what the score during the scrimmage was, their communication would always be clear, direct, and with a purpose. Their communication would include the name of the person and what they wanted that person to do, like "Suzie, slide right." In the first scrimmage their communication was more along the lines of "Someone cover her" or "I need help over here."

The fourth battle was to string together three offensive passes in a row. In the first scrimmage the girls were unable to attack offensively; they were paralyzed by fear. In the first scrimmage if Courtney's team had the ball in scoring position it was usually one girl on offense against four girls on defense. They realized if they could make three passes in a row, they would set up scoring opportunities.

The next scrimmage Courtney's girls played much better and lost by a score of 3-1. Knowing how the national champions dominated their games, Courtney's girls were never so happy about a 3-1 loss. The scrimmages were only two days apart!

Overtraining

Sean Killion, 1992 U.S. Olympic Swim Team member, experienced overtraining. His freshman year at Cal, Sean swam three seconds slower in his best event, the 500-yard freestyle, than he swam in high school. Sean had trained very hard his freshman year at Cal and could not understand why he swam slower at the end of the year. Athletes like Sean, who are capable of very intense training, are frequently overtrained. It is often hard to moderate training for someone who, like Sean, was willing to run through a brick wall for success. Sean quickly recovered from being overtrained and five months later broke the American Record in the 800-meter freestyle by six seconds.

Coaches must be very careful with athletes who are willing

> A good athlete learns to listen to his or her body. Coaches should not be quick to look for mental excuses when an athlete does not perform well; many times there is a physical explanation for a poor performance.

to do everything the coach asks. In many sports these athletes end up exhausted. By not being allowed to recover, they literally train themselves out of shape. Sometimes coaches must hold athletes back because many athletes will do more training on their own after practice.

Often a psychological explanation is given for the athlete's failure. Sean said, "I thought for a minute, perhaps I could not succeed at the college level, but deep down I knew the reason I did not swim fast was outside of me." Sean had experienced enough success prior to his freshman year of college to know something external was going on.

Unfortunately, too many athletes and coaches blame the athlete's poor mental skills for their failure. Before athletes are overtrained they usually have done some great things either in competition or in practice. However, as the season progresses, they do not rest and recover, thus they get worse. A good athlete learns to listen to his or her body. Coaches should not be quick to look for mental excuses when an athlete does not perform well; many times there is a physical explanation for a poor performance.

Building Self-Confidence

Here are some steps to build self-confidence in your athletes.

Step 1. Know what you are doing. As a coach, you need to know what it is going to take for your athletes to succeed. This involves knowing what skill you want them to learn and knowing how to teach that skill.

Step 2. Create an environment where the athlete has to succeed. No matter what you are trying to teach, make it so easy that each athlete will be able to successfully do the task. You want them to practice and learn the skill; thus, your instruction should start so simple that they have to succeed. An athlete must be able to do a skill with no pressure in order to do the same skill under intense pressure. Praise the athletes for their success.

Step 3. Gradually raise the bar. Once the athletes have learned the skill properly, ask them to do it on a regular basis. Do not get caught up in results. For example, in a sport where athletes need to modify or change their grip, technique, or stance, success should be measured by their ability to implement their new skill. Too many athletes do not make changes because when they do make a change they perform worse, at first. By lowering your expectations, it lowers the pressure on the athlete to perform. Praise them for their change.

Step 4. Keep the focus on doing the technique properly. No matter what you are trying to teach the athletes, focus on their technique. Proper technique will lead to good results in the long run. Praise them for their success.

Step 5. For athletes over the age of twelve, once they have learned the proper technique, increase the pressure on them. Gradually create pressure situations in practice that simulate games. Here are some drills I have seen used—in basketball, have each player take the role of shooting a basket as the clock is ticking down. Have the rest of the team watch and cheer and count down the seconds before the shot. First this can be done with nobody guarding the shooter, next the defense is loosely guarding the shooter, finally, the defense is trying to stop the shooter from scoring. Also, each player could shoot two free throws, with no time on the clock and the team down by one point.

In golf—set up a tough, but make-able putt. Have each

player take his or her turn at making the putt while the rest of the team cheers or tries to distract the putter.

In tennis—have two players play against one. The goal is for the two players to make the other player run as much as possible. Thus, they try to hit the ball just out of the reach of the single player. After everyone has done this drill, they all will be surprised at the balls they were able to return.

In swimming, create a stress day. On the stress day there is a stress set. Back off in training intensity for a day or two before the stress day. On the stress set, give each athlete a goal time. Make it reachable, but very hard. We used to say, "You need to go five swims at the time we gave you; take as much rest as you need. You will do five swims at that time or better. You may make it in five tries, you may make it in ten; but we know you can do this if you put your mind to it." Post the results; give out gold stars or some other reward.

In soccer—some tips from Bay Area standout coach Owen Flannery. Owen states, "I have my players take penalty kicks in practice. I break the team into two even teams and have them sit in their groups on each side of the field. When one of the players is about to shoot her penalty kick, I tell her if she makes the shot no one will run, but if she misses the shot, her teammates will have to sprint across the field. Also, while still broken into two teams, I have the offensive team play like they are winning by one goal and I have the defensive team high press them. This drill trains both the offense and defense to play all out. I tell both groups that if they make a mistake the other team will tie them. There is always a reward for the winning team. With this type of drill I train my girls to learn how to play with a lead, because it is often very hard for teams to execute properly when they have the lead if they have not done so under pressure in a practice situation."

The goal with each of these drills is to make the pressure

so intense in practice that the game seems easier. Athletes' self-confidence develops when they can see the progress they have made. Too many coaches try to go directly to this step without gradually bringing the athlete along; by doing so they increase failure and actually decrease the athlete's self-confidence.

Step 6. Tell the athletes you believe in them. As a coach your views and beliefs carry a lot of weight. Individually, let your athletes know the progress you have seen them make. Tell them how good you think they can be. Every athlete has doubts; when you praise them for their successes and then tell them they can continue to succeed, their doubts decrease and their self-confidence grows.

CHAPTER 10

John's Son—High School Basketball

MPI (www.mpi-treatment.org) is the name of the Chemical Dependency Treatment Center where I work part time. Occasionally, in my work with addicts and alcoholics, I talk about sports. I tell those in treatment that many athletes succeed because they see themselves succeeding. By the same token, those in treatment should be able to see themselves living life clean and sober when they leave a structured treatment program.

After a group session, one of the clients, John, came up to talk to me. At times people come to our treatment program from outside the San Francisco Bay Area. John traveled to our Oakland program from the Los Angeles area. He was going home the next day and desperately wanted to talk about his son. I invited him to my office and we spent a little time together.

Terry, John's sixteen-year-old son, was a high school basketball player. When Terry was in eighth grade, the coach of his high school team, Ron, told Terry he would get a lot of playing time if he came to his team. Coach Ron assured Terry that he would start for sure by his sophomore year. He stated he had connections and could help the young man secure a Division One basketball scholarship.

As a sophomore Terry was the seventh or eighth man on the varsity team. He would get some playing time, but it never amounted to much. At the end of his sophomore year Terry was thinking of transferring to another school. Coach Ron was upset about this and told Terry if he stayed, he would definitely be a starter next year.

Terry decided to stay with Coach Ron for his junior year but things were about the same for Terry as they were his sophomore year. He started for a game or two; then Coach Ron would switch the lineup around. This made no sense to Terry's father because at times Terry would score sixteen points and get eight rebounds in one game, then would barely get to play in the next game. There seemed to be no rhyme or reason to Coach Ron's decisions.

John said, "I know I'm his dad, but the kid can play. Many other parents have asked me why Terry is not getting more playing time." John also talked about some of the things Terry told him about playing for Coach Ron. Terry said, even though Coach Ron was married, he brought his girlfriend along on out-of-town games. Coach Ron said the team was a family, and, "Like a family, we don't talk about our problems with others." Coach Ron was talking about a dysfunctional family.

Bringing the girlfriend to away games was not the only concern. It seems Coach Ron was probably an alcoholic as he and his girlfriend would get very drunk at these out-of-town games. Terry was very discouraged about the past three years and set up an appointment to talk with Coach Ron. This was after the end of his junior season. Terry was once again thinking of transferring.

Terry had talked with his dad about his limited playing time and neither of them knew what to do about the situation. They decided it would be best for Terry to have a heart-to-heart talk with Coach Ron. Terry and his dad prepared in detail what Terry would say to Coach Ron.

Terry talked to Coach Ron and they agreed to meet the following morning during first period—around 8:00 A.M. Terry was very nervous when he showed up at Coach Ron's office. He was surprised to see the lights out, but knocked anyway, and heard Coach Ron ask, "Who is it?" Terry opened the door and saw Coach Ron lying on the floor, trying to sleep off another hangover. Coach Ron asked Terry to come back some other time. He did not even seem to remember that Terry was going to come by to talk with him. Terry and his dad were very confused. They had no idea what to do, which is why John wanted to talk to me—he wanted me to make the decision for them.

In chemical dependency treatment we often talk about the concept of insanity. We define insanity as doing the same thing over and over, but expecting different results each time. There is a lot of insanity in chemical dependency. People get treatment, then leave, and later think they will now be able to handle drinking. They do the same behavior—drink—and expect a different result—being able to handle it. This never works. If they are lucky they may make it back into treatment, but all too often they end up dead.

We do not use the word insane describing them, but insane clearly describes their repetitive alcoholic behavior pattern. I am reminded of a good friend of mine who was an assistant swim coach at a Division One college. The head coach was trying to print something from the computer. He printed the document, held it up, and said, "The margins aren't right." The coach did not change anything. He just hit print again, and of course, got the same result. The coach picked up the document and said, "The margins aren't right on this one either." He did the same thing a third and fourth time too, and by now my friend was dying laughing. My friend said, "Hey coach, why don't you hit print a fifth time, maybe the margins will fix themselves."

> We define insanity as doing the same thing over and over, but expecting different results each time.

The man was a perfectly sane and logical coach; however, attempting to change the margins by just hitting print is without sanity. This example of human behavior in other venues should be recognized first, then avoided.

I pointed out to John that both he and Terry were expecting a different result from Coach Ron. Coach Ron had lied to both of them for years; to expect him to change as Terry approached his senior year fits our definition of insanity.

I told John that I understood Terry's friends were important. However, he and Terry had to face the facts. If basketball was not that important to Terry, he should stay at the same high school. If basketball was really important to Terry, it was time to transfer. I suggested to John that he and Terry sit down and talk with each other about staying at the same school or transferring to a new school. I said it was best to leave Coach Ron out of the decision.

Of course, waiting in the wings was another high school basketball coach, hoping Terry would transfer to his team. John knew the coach of this other team and had already talked with him. The coach had two very good juniors returning for next season and would have a great team next year. The person who played Terry's position was graduating and had already signed a scholarship with a Division One school. If Terry transferred, he could be a starter for a very good team.

I told John that Terry had to decide if he wanted to stay with his friends his senior year, or play basketball. I emphasized if he stayed with Coach Ron nothing would change. Terry had to decide how important basketball was his senior year of high school. I could not make the decision—but my recommendation was to get as far away from Coach Ron as possible. I pointed out Coach Ron would not change. If Terry was really serious about basketball and wanted to play in college, he should transfer. There was no way he could play for Coach Ron another year and then go on to play in college, Coach Ron would not play Terry as much because he had probably made the same promises to other kids and would play them. It was quite clear to me that Coach Ron had given up on Terry.

There are times when I meet with people and I never see them again. When this happens, I often wonder, "What happened?" John went back down to Los Angeles the next day, and I did not expect to hear from him ever again.

As it turned out, one year later John called me. John said he had one year clean and sober and wanted to come up to the treatment center to get his one-year sobriety chip. I asked, "Whatever happened with your son and basketball?" John replied, "Oh, you wouldn't believe it. Terry switched schools. He started for the new team and they went on to win the state championship. It was a fantastic experience for him—he is going to play for a Division Two team next year." Terry ended up a "saved egg."

CHAPTER 11

Paul—An NFL Player

I should warn the reader that like many stories in chemical dependency, this one does not have a good ending. Through my work in the field of chemical dependency, I have worked with some professional athletes. The following is one such story.

Paul was a NFL defensive back, referred to me because he was in the NFL's Substance Abuse Program. He did not play for one of the local teams, but because he lived in the area and spent most of his time here, he was referred to me. He was in the NFL's substance abuse program because of a positive marijuana test.

In the field of chemical dependency we constantly deal with the defense mechanism of denial—this means denial of reality. There are many aspects of denial, some healthy, some unhealthy. Healthy denial, for many of us here in California, is the denial of the possibility of another major earthquake. We have prepared as best we can, but on a daily basis we do not think that the building we are in will collapse, or that we will die in the next hour or so. If we thought like this we would never go into a big building; we would simply wait in a large empty field for the "big one."

Unhealthy denial is what we see in chemical dependency. Once, doing an assessment for chemical dependency, I asked a person, "How many DUI's (driving under the influence) have you had?" His reply was, "Well let's see, one this year, three in the 1990s. I had those three in the 1980s—and I think I had a few in the 1970s, so probably about ten all together." I then asked, "Do you feel like you are an alcoholic?" He replied, "No, I just have bad luck with the cops when I drive."

Denial in addiction can be about the severity of the addiction, or the denial can be about what is necessary to do to stay clean and sober. The alcoholic who upon leaving treatment says, "Oh, I'll be all right, I have no desire to drink again, I don't need to go to AA [Alcoholics Anonymous] meetings, I just won't drink," is in serious denial and heading for trouble. He or she may not be in denial about being an alcoholic, but he or she is in denial about what it will take to stay clean and sober.

The last person whom I had worked with who had a similar denial problem had just died from acute alcohol poisoning. After this person had received his third DUI, he served about six months in jail. By then, he had lost his job, his wife left him, and his kids refused to speak to him. Yet, this person, on a downward spiral, was convinced that he did not have a problem with alcohol at all. Even other alcoholics would say, "Man, that guy is in serious denial." I could tell that Paul's denial was just as severe.

How I work with an addict in denial is much different than how I would work with any athlete. When someone is in denial, I bring up reality, to confront the denial. With many athletes I may use a kinder, gentler approach. This approach does not work with addicts. It is necessary to be blunt with them to confront their denial.

Paul was recently out of college and had been drafted in a late round of the NFL draft. He was not a high profile player, but just another guy struggling for playing time. He was, like many NFL players, a guy people do not notice when they join or leave a team because they are in the shadows of the superstars and are scraping by to make a career. These players of course still get drug tested. Paul's positive test for marijuana was what brought him in to see me.

At the time of our first meeting, Paul was still smoking marijuana daily. He said he had not signed the contract for the Substance Abuse Program and he would smoke marijuana up until the minute he signed the contract. He said that he had already lost $200,000 because of his positive drug test, which was money he desperately needed. However, as I came to understand Paul's exaggerations, it became clearer the amount of money lost might have been significantly less.

Paul said that marijuana did not impair him at all, in fact, marijuana made him play video games better. He said that the NFL's rule on substance abuse was stupid and that he would stop using when he had to stop to comply, but he did not think he had a drug problem at all. He reported he had one DUI in the past, but should have had six or eight. He claimed that being a professional football player he could talk his way out of a DUI. I did not know if this was true or not. As you will see, his denial cut across all areas of his life, and he thought he was a much bigger deal that he actually was. He claimed that alcohol did not impair him either. I later realized the reason alcohol did not impair him was because he was using speed at the same time.

In our first session, it was clear to me that Paul thought he knew everything; he did not feel like he had a problem or needed help. He acted as if he was there to see me for my benefit and I should be honored to be meeting with him. My reply to him at the end of our first session was, "I think you are full of it."

After our first session and after having Paul sign the necessary releases, I was in contact with the NFL's representative. The way things were set up Paul needed to meet with me two times per week; he also needed to go to two AA or NA (Narcotics Anonymous) meetings per week. I told both the NFL and Paul that it was my recommendation that Paul do a 28-day inpatient chemical dependency treatment program. If he would not agree to do inpatient treatment, then he should do outpatient treatment. I suspected he would not agree to do any treatment, but I felt I should make my recommendation known.

We met for the second time on a Friday. By then the NFL had faxed me Paul's treatment plan, which I went over with him. Paul said he wanted a treatment plan under a psychologist who understood he did not have a drug problem. He said that since we all knew he was in the substance abuse program, we were biased against him and wrongfully believed he was a drug addict. He wanted the option to see someone that was not already biased, with the hope this psychologist would say he did not have a problem with alcohol or drugs. I think this was Paul's way to try to stall signing the contract, as he never brought this issue up again after he signed the contract.

Paul told me he wanted to take the NFL's treatment plan home so he could talk it over with his wife, then sign it when he returned to see me on Monday. To anyone who has ever worked in chemical dependency, this statement means, "I want to get loaded one more weekend." Before Paul left my office that Friday, he told me he was still high from using crank the night before.

Crank is methamphetamine, a stimulant. In the past it was called speed; it can be smoked, snorted, or injected. Paul liked to snort crank while drinking alcohol because he could drink much more alcohol when using crank. The high from crank can last many hours and Paul liked to play football while high on crank too.

Our next session was three days later, on Monday. Paul came in and we went over his contract from the NFL. We also went over my recommendations for chemical dependency treatment. He signed his contract then told me he had smoked marijuana on the way to my office. He said this was all right, because, after all, he had not signed the contract yet. Normally, I would not meet with someone who was high; I would send him away. I still talked with Paul after he signed the contract. I figured we were both there and might as well try to get something done.

Paul began to talk about problems he had with people. Often, he did not get along with his coaches. He said he had been drafted in a late round because of his attitude. No one really doubted his ability to play. He clearly had talent, but teams were worried he would be more trouble than he was worth. He had problems in college with his coaches and he had been arrested for drugs too. Perhaps this is what he was referring to when he said he had lost $200,000 from drug-related issues.

Paul reported that his father was an alcoholic. He remembered being young and helping carry his father into the house when his father was drunk. He had two older brothers, both of whom were alcoholics; he also had a younger sister who smoked a lot of weed. When Paul was in college his father used to call at all hours of the night, drunk, wanting to talk with Paul.

His dad would try to take credit for the success Paul achieved. Recently, Paul was at a bar with his dad—both drunk, Paul told his dad he had absolutely no respect for him at all, as little respect as a son could have for a father.

As we began to meet, Paul talked more and more about his dad. He said that his whole life his father tried to live off of Paul's success and glory. His father used to say things like "When you make it big, you'll buy us a new house, right?" His dad used to talk about what kind of car he wanted Paul to buy him when Paul hit the big time.

As a child, Paul was never able to express his feelings to his father, primarily because his dad was drunk most of the time. He kept his feelings toward his father bottled up inside. As time went on, Paul became more and more self-destructive.

As we began to meet, I looked into Paul's extensive drug history. One thing that stood out the most was his extensive use of LSD. In his life, primarily in high school and college, he had used LSD over 200 times. LSD is a hallucinogenic; it changes how you perceive things and it was a popular drug back in the 1960s. My experience working in the field of chemical dependency is that LSD really affects the user's thought process. Empirically I have found that when someone comes into treatment who has done a lot of acid, his or her thought process is muddled. They have a hard time connecting the dots; they are very tangential. They start talking about something that leads to something else and they keep going on and on. They may get around to explaining an idea but it looks like their brain connections are not firing properly. An example of this would be if I asked someone who has used a lot of LSD, "When did you last smoke marijuana?" Their reply might be something like: "Well, let's see, I was going up to San Francisco to a party, traffic was bad, you know when traffic gets bad on the bridge, well I was stuck in traffic like that, I was with my cousin, he's from San Diego, he came to visit me because I went down to see him three weeks ago, when we were kids we used to play baseball together, I used to be a pitcher. I wanted to be like Nolan Ryan, I saw him play once,…" You get the picture. They are not psychotic, out of touch with reality; however, their brain does not seem to process things like the brains of those that have not done LSD.

Paul was what we call a polysubstance abuser, or what drug addicts call a garbage can addict. Garbage can addicts will use any drug they can get their hands on. Paul had done them all, especially lots of marijuana and alcohol since high school. In college he used cocaine, speed, and opiates. About the only drug Paul had not used was heroin.

Like some professional athletes I have dealt with, Paul thought the world revolved around him. When I called ten minutes after he was supposed to be at our appointment he told me he "would take a shower and then come over." In the sessions right after he signed the contract, he was extremely upset about being in the NFL's Substance Abuse Program. He felt like everyone, including me (especially me), was out to get him. He could not see his role in this process at all—he was a victim of stupid rules. Throughout his life Paul's view was "me against the world."

As we progressed, I tried to point out a theme in his life; everything was Paul versus them. Those of us working with him now were just the new people he was fighting against. Recently he fought with his pro coaches, who, according to Paul, were not playing him because he didn't kiss up to them. In college he didn't get along with his coaches because "They were out to get me because of my attitude."

Paul had gone to a few AA and NA meetings. He saw those who went to AA or NA meetings as weak people who can't handle drugs; they became another one of Paul's them. He was not one of them (addicts); he could handle drugs. According to Paul he didn't have a problem with drugs; he had a problem with stupid rules.

It was during this time that Paul told me he had been cut from his NFL team. He then told me that the reason he had been cut may have been because the week before the season ended he missed curfew and missed a practice. This was not the first time he had broken the team's rules. He also had a problem with his position coach, who did not like him for some mysterious reason. Paul could not see that his behavior had anything to do with getting cut or his current circumstances. Actually his denial level bordered on the incredible.

Through all this turmoil, Paul's agent was in contact with other teams. Paul clearly had talent; other teams had shown interest in signing him. His agent told the new teams that Paul had a personality conflict with his position coach. The agent also told Paul that when they meet with a representative from any team, Paul was to keep his mouth shut. The agent told Paul, "You talk too much."

During this time Paul had a request. When the NFL's national representative came and the three of us met, Paul said he wanted to meet with me three times per week, rather than the two sessions we were now doing. Paul suggested this so he would not have to go to NA or AA meetings. I was beginning to doubt if he was going to meetings at all, so I gave him a sheet to have signed at the meetings to prove he went—I never saw the sheet again.

My frustrations were beginning to grow and I was wondering if I could continue to work with Paul, because our sessions were turning into arguments. I was trying to convince him he had a problem and he was trying to give me speeches about how he can handle drugs and alcohol. I had given him an article each session on some aspect of chemical dependency or drug research; I doubt he ever even looked at any of these.

There is one problem here that I often see in athletes. I see that sometimes their greatest strength can also be their greatest weakness. For Paul, his strength was that he did everything all by himself. The way he got to this position in life was by the work he did and the talent he had. Naturally, he thought coaches had no role in his success; his self-reliance was his strength. He was a do-it-yourself kind of guy. This is a huge weakness in recovery; the first word of the 12 steps of AA is "We." "We," meaning, not "I." In other words you must have the help and support of others for a successful recovery program. Paul was used to doing things all by himself. Self-reliance in this case would be his downfall. In chemical dependency we talk about surrendering, not trying to work your own program. Because Paul had experienced success on his own, he was not about to surrender and do what others told him to do—even if it cost him his career.

This concept of surrender is very important in recovery. Surrender means you quit fighting and do what is suggested in order to live a clean and sober life. The concept of surrender was foreign to Paul; he could not envision surrendering to anything. He felt that if he wanted to do something, he could do it. In his mind, if he chose to quit using drugs and alcohol, he could stop; he just never chose to quit. In his mind, he was a recreational user.

The same mindset that got him to the professional ranks was going to destroy him. I feel this is at the heart of why many professional athletes cannot stay clean and sober. They had their success by their own doing; they feel they can get off drugs by their own self-will and determination. Unfortunately, things seldom, if ever, work out that way.

The idea that one's strength is also a weakness cuts across many areas of a person's life. The guy or girl who can shut off his or her emotions in sports may have a hard time turning them on in a relationship, and may seem emotionally unresponsive. The person with a lot of self-confidence may not notice if he or she needs some extra help or if things are getting off track.

Paul was heading for trouble and it did not take long for problems to occur. He told me he went to a party and had about seven glasses of wine. My experience in chemical dependency is that everyone under-reports his or her use. For him to tell me he had seven glasses of wine means he had so much to drink, he could not remember how much he drank. A realistic guess about how

> The idea that one's strength is also a weakness cuts across many areas of a person's life. The guy or girl who can shut off his or her emotions in sports may have a hard time turning them on in a relationship, and may seem emotionally unresponsive. The person with a lot of self-confidence may not notice if he or she needs some extra help or if things are getting off track.

much he drank would have been between seven and seventeen glasses of wine.

I told Paul I had to let the proper people know that he drank. I also said it was obvious to me that he had not been going to AA meetings. He told me he decided that he did not need AA, that he could stop on his own, and that after all, he was not an alcoholic or a drug addict anyway. This decision that AA meetings were not for him came after going to two meetings. The more I saw Paul, the more I felt like I was talking to a wall. We were wasting each other's time.

I tried to get him to come up with an estimate of how much money he had spent on alcohol and drugs in his life. This was one of the things I used to do at the treatment center where I work. It is often an eye-opening experience for individuals to calculate how much money their drug use has cost them. In calculating the total cost of their use, I would have them include cost of buying the alcohol or drugs, cost for legal fees, missed work, accidents, and gas money used to go to purchase alcohol or drugs. I had them include any cost incurred as a result of their alcohol and drug use. I would even have them include buying drinks at a bar for others and tips given to the bartender.

Calculating the financial damage from drug use seems to work well with those who are money oriented. Paul was money oriented. Many professional football players make the big bucks, as he put it, even though he did not. He still owed his father about $20,000 because he had let Paul borrow money to help him get situated before he signed the big contract. Getting drafted in the middle to late rounds often does not lead to a big contract. Many of these late round draft picks end up getting cut; they never make the big bucks.

Paul calculated that he had spent at least $19,000 on alcohol and drugs during the past year. This was money that he could have used to repay his father or used for other reasons, but he was convinced the big contract was right around the corner and that $19,000 was not much money at all.

With Paul getting cut from his team, the prospect of the big money was getting more and more remote. His dad, while drunk, called Paul and said, "That's the last time I put all my eggs in your basket."

Paul talked about the fact that when he used LSD he was able to create his own world. I tried to point out this was what he was trying to do now, without using LSD. The reality of his world now was that his future in the NFL looked bleak at best. Also, alcohol and drugs had substantially impacted his life. He needed to go to AA and NA meetings and embrace a recovery program. He had not been working out and was not in shape. His attitude toward his coaches needed to become a lot more positive.

Paul was entrenched in his denial. He saw me the same as he saw most other people. I did not understand him, or football. His view was "I can play and that's all that matters." He said, "If I was a star offensive player this would not matter at all, but being a grunt defensive back, everyone is out to get me and make an example out of me."

Despite our lack of measurable progress, meeting three times per week was challenging and interesting. Surprisingly, Paul started showing up early for our sessions. Also, at the end of 50 minutes he would ask if we could keep talking and would act upset when I said, "No, it can wait two days." I told him about my experience working with him and said, "You put people off. When we first started meeting you put me off, everything has to be you against them, then once you open up and start talking, you're really not a bad guy at all." I really felt this was true and his tough guy image was a way to keep people at bay to protect himself from getting hurt. Anytime he let people get close to him, like his father, Paul ended up hurt. I pointed out that this was why he had problems with coaches and why he does not want to give anyone from AA or NA an opportunity to get to know him.

Paul told me that he recently got a letter from his defensive back coach from his college team. While in college they did not get along; they had a personality conflict, as Paul saw it. His coach wrote to him and said, in his twenty-five years of coaching, Paul was the most talented athlete he had ever coached. The coach stated that Paul's attitude was his downfall and that he hoped Paul would realize this and change. He had heard Paul had been cut and he felt that if Paul could change his attitude all his NFL dreams would come true.

I wish I could say that the letter from his coach had a big impact on Paul—it did not. Paul was glad to get the letter, but all he saw was the part about talent. He did not think he needed to change at all. He thought that perhaps the coach "wanted me to put in a good word for him in the NFL."

Paul and I continued to meet but he continued to try to do things his way. He rarely, if ever, went to AA or NA meetings, and he began to drink more often. He figured if he did not use marijuana he was in compliance with the NFL.

Paul ended up getting a tryout with a team and was with them for a little while. During this time we talked by phone. Paul, as usual, had conflicts with his new coaches, and was soon cut. The day he was cut he went out and smoked marijuana. Another team expressed interest in him. Paul told them he had smoked marijuana, because after all, he had been cut and was not under the NFL's rules anymore in his eyes. The other team said they would not pursue signing Paul because of his drug use.

Paul was once again the victim. He could justify smoking marijuana because he was not on a team at the time he smoked. His agent told him that there was nothing he could do for Paul anymore and that his career was over. His agent said he was damaged goods, and that Paul was not trying to change his life at all so no team wanted him. Thus, Paul's professional football career ended—actually it never really began.

CHAPTER 12

Tips for Clinicians

Define What You Do

As a clinician, you need to provide something that is separate from what the coach provides and you should be able to articulate what it is you have to offer. A competent clinician offers more than goal setting, relaxation, visualization, and motivation because most good coaches do these things. Keep in mind that most coaches are very protective of their athletes. You must be able to show the coach that you have something to add that they either do not do, or do not have the time to do.

Take Pressure off the Athlete

Your focus should be to help take pressure off athletes. They often have pressure from coaches, parents, teammates, and especially from themselves. Most of the time when someone wants to quit it is because the pressure is overwhelming. You need to provide a realistic approach to everyone's expectations because unrealistic expectations are one of the primary sources of pressure.

I have worked with many young athletes in their freshman or sophomore year of high school. Often they want to quit because the pressure is so great, they would much rather hang out with their friends. These first two years of high school are really a crucial time in sports because if athletes quit at this time, it is very hard for them to come back. The reason kids want to quit is because there is no more joy or fun in the sport. When their athletic careers should be beginning to bloom, these athletes are burning out. Their coaches pressure them constantly. Their parents expect them to do well in both school and in sports. The pressure to get into a good college is already building. These young athletes begin to ask, "What about me?—When is my time to have fun? I have been at this for eight years now and I want a break."

These athletes often do not really want to quit; they simply see no other option to deal with the pressure and they do not really think through the decision to quit. I had one young guy come to see me because he wanted to quit the basketball team. He was starting his sophomore year of high school. His father, who had been his basketball coach in middle school, was so upset that his son wanted to quit the team, he took a day off from work. I spoke with both him and his wife on the phone before meeting with their son. His dad was distraught, telling me his son had been a great athlete since second grade and now was throwing it all away. He had already thought of colleges where his son could play and even had dreams of his son playing professional basketball. The dad pleaded with me to get his son to change his mind. I told him, "I am not going to try to convince him to play, but I will talk with him about the decision. I will gladly see him, but the decision to play or not is his." I said this because otherwise the kid would think, "Dad can't deal with me quitting—so he is taking me to a 'shrink' so he can try to convince me to play."

When the young man came in I explained the decision to play or not was his alone, but I stressed that "I think this

> These athletes often do not really want to quit; they simply see no other option to deal with the pressure and they do not really think through the decision to quit.

is an important decision, and I think we should talk about your decision." He began to talk about all the pressure he felt. He had been one of the best players on the freshman team the previous year. He had gone out for the cross-country team his freshman year to help with his conditioning for basketball. He was about the sixth to eighth runner on the cross-country team. He did not want to go to the Championship meet at the end of the season, as the cross-country team was just fun for him. When he told the coach he wanted to go to a basketball camp that weekend instead of the cross-country Championship, the coach went ballistic. The coach told him, "If you don't run at the Championships, you will never run at this school again and I will do my best to see that you are kept off the basketball team as well." This made no sense to him as they only scored the top four runners at the Championships and he had never been in the top four. The coach stressed a commitment to the team, but this kid was committed to his basketball team. He went to the cross-country Championships and finished sixth out of the eight runners on his team. His coach pretty much ignored him during the Championships. He was resentful and angry at his coach's treatment of him. He felt like "If this is what high school sports are all about, then I don't want any part of them."

As far as basketball, in his sophomore year the coaches were already talking about having him play on the varsity team. The varsity team was very good, meaning he probably would not get much playing time his sophomore year. Some of the other guys from the freshman team quit and were enjoying their free time away from practice. The more he talked with me in the session, the more he realized he loved basketball, but he hated the pressure that came with his high school's sports program. Previously, he had fused basketball and pressure together in his mind. I asked him, "Under what conditions would you play?" He said, "There are two issues. First, if my dad quits bugging me about basketball—it's all we talk about. He needs to back off and just let me play. The other way I would play is if my dad does not come to my games—he is constantly yelling from the sidelines and it embarrasses me."

When I got him to talk about what he loved about basketball, his face lit up as he began to talk about his teammates and the fun they had both on and off the court. I pointed out that if he quit as a sophomore it would be very hard to come back as a junior or even a senior. He said, "Well I might play in college." I explained how hard it would be to play in college if he did not play his last three years of high school. Once again, he had not thought this decision through.

> Successful athletes are usually harder on themselves than anyone else. You should help them to realize that they often have unrealistic expectations and being so hard on themselves actually hurts their performance.

I asked him if he felt comfortable telling his dad under what conditions he would play. He was unsure about this, as he knew how much basketball meant to his dad. We went over ways to talk to his dad about these conditions. As we were wrapping up I asked him if he could take a couple days to think about his decision. I told him it would be best to think it over for a few days, then make the decision. He agreed; a few days later he called me and told me he decided to play. We only met one time.

In my experience, the more success athletes have, the more pressure they often feel. A good clinician should provide a place where they can talk about the mounting pressures. As Matt Biondi described it, "It was one thing getting to the top; it's a different ball game trying to stay there." Successful athletes are usually harder on themselves than anyone else. You should help them to realize that they often have unrealistic expectations and being so hard on themselves actually hurts their performance.

197

Be a Guide

You should show the athletes the way to success. This may sound trite, but when many athletes seek help they are in a quagmire and see no way out. Let them know that there is a way out, because there almost always is. Tell them, "If we work on A, B, C, and D, and you do 1, 2, 3, and 4 you will be fine." This is frequently very reassuring to athletes because when they come to see you, they are often paralyzed from being totally overwhelmed. Being overwhelmed keeps them from seeing clearly what they need to do, because they are often very confused. Your main focus should simply be solving the question, "What do you need to do to improve your game?" If you keep this in mind, you can help guide them to improve their performances.

Look at Good and Bad

Too often athletes do not want to look at the bad performances, but there are volumes of information in both the good and bad performances. Make sure you go over what happened, in detail, during both good and bad performances. I usually start a few days after these performances and see what was going on. You should focus on what they were thinking, feeling, and experiencing during this whole time. When you break these things down, it is much easier to see patterns in their performance. I always have athletes describe in detail for me both their best and worst performances.

If you do not look at athletes' bad performances there could be big problems. I feel that too many athletes try to move on after a bad performance. If they do not process these performances, the next time that same situation comes around they are in big trouble. In some states the big competitions are held at the same venue each year and if players had a bad performance the year before at the big game, when they walk in that same place a year later they will think, "last time I was here I choked."

They need to process what went wrong and why; otherwise they will not understand why they had a bad performance last year.

Shift Skills

Shift what they already do because most of the time you do not need to teach someone a new skill. By looking back at an athlete's best performances, you can find out what worked. Then you look at what they did there, when it worked, and figure out how they can do that here, when it is not working. What I mean by this is that often athletes have had success and by focusing on what worked for them, it is much easier for them to implement what they have already done. Thus, you are not teaching them something foreign to them, you are identifying what went right and wrong and why things happened that way. If athletes can't clearly see the reasons for their success or failure, they will become superstitious and think that because they wore their lucky hat they won.

When you have an understanding of why athletes have a good performance and why they have a bad performance, it clears the picture up; then they see all of the things that happen when things went well. For example, many athletes think they need to be fired up and they think that by being emotionally charged up, it means they are ready to perform. Often when you examine the details of a performance, you see that their best performances were when they were relaxed and calm and felt no pressure. Then you take these feelings, relaxed and calm, and transfer them to the other performances. At the same time you help them remove the belief that they have to be fired up. Look at where this idea came from and help them realize that while it is something many people say—in reality it may not be a good idea. When fired up many people are over-stimulated and do not focus or think clearly. They are like a deer in your headlights.

Show How

Knowing what to do is not enough; many clinicians get frustrated because athletes know what they need to do, yet they are not doing it: "I know I shouldn't think 'what if I miss this putt,' but I can't help it." Athletes need to be taught **how** to do the things they need to do. Teaching how to change is one of your primary tasks. Athletes need to learn to focus on what they want to have happen, instead of what they do not want to have happen. You need to be able to teach them how to improve their confidence, change their thoughts, relax, and limit the impact of their coach or parents on their self-esteem.

Usually by the time athletes come to see you they have been told what they need to do by everyone, but they do not know how to make the necessary changes. This is also true in chemical dependency. Almost everyone who comes into treatment knows he or she needs to stop using drugs and alcohol but has no idea how to stop, which is why so many addicts relapse. They come to treatment to get off drugs, but they have no idea how to stay off drugs. I often tell them, "There are two issues here, one, getting off drugs, and two, staying off drugs. Getting off is simple; we don't even concern ourselves with this short-term goal, but it is a lifelong process to stay off drugs." Often people who use opiates say, "All you have to do is get me off. I can't stop on my own because of the withdrawal symptoms, but once I am off, I'll never go back." The reason they rarely stay clean and sober is twofold. First of all, they think they know what is best for them, when actually they have no clue. Secondly, they don't take into account how incredibly hard it is to change a lifelong pattern of behavior. Their drug has been their only successful way to cope with life. Once off drugs, they need to learn how to deal with problems without using drugs as their coping mechanism.

The same is true for athletes; you need to show them how to change. They did not come to you for the solution, they already know it; they came to see you so you can show them how to implement the solution.

Transition

Remember there will be a transition phase for change to occur. Most college coaches will tell you it is hard to have a freshman come in and have an impact right away. The coach has to change bad habits that have become ingrained. This is why most college athletes do much better their sophomore, junior, and senior years. The athletes you work with will be the same but it will take time to change patterns of behavior that have been ingrained. Have them put aside the idea that by just seeing you improvement should occur instantly.

I tell parents, "This problem will not change overnight; during the transition phase we should see higher highs and shorter lows." What I mean by this is, they will still have their bad moments, but they will be shorter in duration and not as severe as in the past.

Boundaries

I had an athlete say, "I know having my dad constantly criticize me is not good, but I don't know how to get him to stop, or to keep his criticism from bothering me." Many times athletes need to learn how to say "no." They will need help in setting clear boundaries. They do not know how to tell their coach, parent, or teammate what they are doing or saying is not helpful to them. With family this is very hard because you are dealing with issues that have been around all of the athlete's life. However, if athletes feel they will perform better without their parents at the competition, then the parents should not attend. If the athletes can talk to their parents and clearly state how they want their parents to act and if the parents agree, then the parents should be allowed to attend the competition.

Also, many times teammates say things that are not helpful. You should have the people you work with look at what they say to others, and then figure out how they can tell teammates their negative comments are not helpful. In high school baseball when someone strikes out, the guys on the bench often make unnecessary comments. They do not seem to realize that what they want to hear from others when they strike out is different from what they say if a teammate strikes out.

You should have clear boundaries as a clinician too. By this I mean, you should know if you should talk about yourself and your experiences or not. Rarely do I self-disclose with clients. I would guess many of my non-sport clients have no idea of my sport background, although I have seen some of these people for years. You should only talk about yourself if it adds to helping your client with his or her issues. If you have a client who has had knee surgery, you do not need to tell him or her about your injuries, because it really does not matter, even if you have had the same surgery. What does matter is that you understand what they are going through and that you can help them with their issues. Just because you went through the same surgery is not enough; your empathy and understanding are what will help them the most.

Put Your Ego Aside

Sometimes it is hard for those working with athletes to put their ego aside, but you should not get caught up in the success or failure of the athletes you are working with. Most times your clients will improve. You should stay in the background. Do not try to take any credit at all for what your athletes accomplish. Their success is for them to enjoy. You do not want to become just another person who is trying to take some of their glory. If you try to take any of their glory, they will resent you on some level and probably quit working with you. You will become just another person in a long line of people who are trying to use the athletes for their own good.

Working with high-profile athletes is a very delicate situation. Because everyone has wanted a piece of the high-profile athlete, he or she will be very emotionally defensive when you meet with them. It will take much longer for trust to develop in your relationship with these athletes. It can also be frustrating working with high-profile athletes because they often simply don't listen. They had their success from their own self-will and often want someone just to agree with them. However, you must confront them when they need confronting and support them when they need support. Over time positive changes can occur.

Compliments

Teach the athletes you work with how to take compliments. I have found most athletes, particularly young women, have a hard time taking compliments. They do not want to seem egotistical, so they tend to brush off compliments. Often they feel that what they did was not good enough. I stress that when someone gives an athlete a compliment, he or she should simply say, "Thank you." They should not discount what someone has to say—even if they think they do not deserve it.

Athletes who are not able to take compliments are the ones that have a lot of negative self-talk. Of course it is good to strive to get better. Taking in praise is one way to help build confidence and self-esteem. By discounting a compliment, an athlete is really saying, "I don't deserve it," which may not be true. If someone takes time to give you a compliment and you don't take it in, you are also saying, "You are too ignorant to know a good performance from a bad performance." This is a very rude approach. A simple "Thanks" is much better. As a clinician, you need to point this out and teach athletes to simply say, "Thank you."

Perfectionism

As a clinician you should always watch out for perfectionism; many athletes will describe themselves as perfectionists. This should be a red flag to the clinician. If a young girl describes herself as a perfectionist, you may want to do an assessment and see if she has an eating disorder, as perfectionism is very common in young girls with eating disorders. Also, most athletes who say they are perfectionists often have negative self-talk. This is because nothing they do is good enough and they only see what they did as wrong. It is always good to strive to improve and do better, but it is detrimental for the athlete to hold him- or herself up to a standard that can never be reached.

Listen

Everyone knows how to talk, but a good listener is rare. I am constantly amazed how much of a difference listening makes. Athletes will seek help for a wide variety of problems. If you listen attentively and really try to understand what is going on with them, you have already helped them—just by listening. Often athletes seek help because everyone tells them what to do, but no one listens to them. If you listen in detail and try really to understand their situation and help them figure out what they need to do, you will be very helpful to them.

Be Thorough

Being thorough follows with being a good listener; the clinician needs to completely understand what is going on psychologically with an athlete. Many people who work with athletes think their primary function is to give advice or to teach the athlete a particular skill. This is part of what you do, but it is by no means all of what you do. You need to get the athletes to explain things to you in as much depth as they possibly can. Too often I see graduate students who brush up against very important issues.

Unfortunately, they do not look deep enough. All they ever end up doing is lightly touching on a whole bunch of very important issues, without going into sufficient depth to understand the problem or to implement any changes.

You should be confident you have something to offer your clients and you should know the key areas to explore. By breaking down everything, the solution often emerges. If you only gloss over things, you never get to the bottom of the problem.

Avoid Intellectualizing

I often have graduate students who are very bright, and since they are so comfortable working on an intellectual level, it is hard for them to avoid intellectualizing. It seems now much of sport psychology is research oriented. In many of the textbooks I have come across there is too much intellectualizing. Your first task is to understand what the athlete is experiencing. Once you understand the problem, then you can look for the solution. The solution comes from examining the athlete's thoughts, feelings, and behaviors. Too often I see clinicians who want to dazzle the athletes they work with and show the athletes how smart they are. They do not pace the client, as we say in therapy. Pacing refers to staying on track with the client, not being on point number ten when the athlete is on point number one. Often an athlete will say something like, "I am getting really nervous before my competition." The sport psychologist jumps right in with, "Let me teach you about relaxation."

I see this as a big mistake, because first you need to gather more information. You need to ask all about the nervousness; find out what is happening, when does it start, what are they nervous about and what specifically are their fears. Also, ask what they have done in the past to try to deal with this nervousness. In almost all cases athletes know they should not be so nervous. By the time they come to see a clinician they have already talked with their coach, parents, and perhaps teammates on how not to be so nervous. They may need to learn more about relaxation, but if you try to teach them relaxation before they feel you understand the whole situation, you have lost their respect and the benefit of your work will be very limited. They will think you do not understand them and they will probably never come back to see you again. I often tell my students, "The goal of the first session is to get a second session." If athletes feel that you understand them and can help them, they will gladly set up a second session. Changing behavior takes time and patience.

As a clinician your task is to understand. If you start to intellectualize and get caught up in concepts you think athletes need to learn first, you are in serious trouble. I have seen too many examples in textbooks that look like the clinician is sticking to his or her own agenda rather than looking at what is in the best interest of the athlete.

Support System

A good clinician will help his or her athletes develop their support system. Remember, you should not be their support system, but part of their support system. Many athletes are reluctant to talk about any problems they have and this is especially true when an athlete is injured. When injured, athletes often do not spend time with the team. They isolate and frequently become depressed. This is a time when they should be doing more talking about what is going on, but is frequently a time when they are doing less talking.

Athletes feel that talking about their injury makes them more depressed. They often think, "What's the use, I'm out for the season anyway." If these are high school or college athletes, they often party more when injured. Drugs or alcohol becomes their coping mechanism for their injury. This is a terrible pattern that commonly occurs.

Some of my graduate students facilitate injured athlete groups at local colleges. Often they have a hard time getting athletes to their groups, even though there are many athletes who are hurt and not playing. Often athletes are reluctant to attend the groups because they do not want to talk about their injury and instead try to move on.

As a clinician your task is to understand. If you start to intellectualize and get caught up in concepts you think athletes need to learn first, you are in serious trouble. I have seen too many examples in textbooks that look like the clinician is sticking to his or her own agenda rather than looking at what is in the best interest of the athlete.

The ancient Greeks defined happiness as using our bodies and our minds to the best of our ability. Injured athletes quit using their bodies and shut down their emotions. Over the years I have had many graduate students who have worked successfully with injured athletes by getting them to talk, doing imagery exercises, and increasing their support system.

You should get athletes to expand their support network. They are often reluctant because they will get asked fifty times a day, "How is your shoulder?" They get tired of people asking the repetitive question. However, there are people they should talk to about their condition. They need to identify those people and talk to them, and ignore the rest. Instead they often ignore everyone and isolate themselves. Their healing will be greatly improved if they expand their support system and gradually open up and talk.

Meanings

You should try to find out what meaning athletes attach to an outcome. If they have a bad performance, find out what their explanation is for the bad showing. Often athletes come up with, "I choked," or some other broad type of statement to blame themselves. Their behavior may have been part of the reason they did poorly, but chances are good there are other reasons. Perhaps they were just playing an opponent who was better than they are, or had bad coaching advice. The important thing is to look at the conclusions they have drawn from their performances and see how to make this a positive step in going forward.

CHAPTER 13

Janet—A Professional Musician

Janet played the cello for one of the local orchestras. She came to see me because she was concerned about her playing. She had been a member of the orchestra for some time now, but thought the quality of her play had been going down lately. Janet was having a lot of anxiety and was experiencing a tremendous amount of stress because of work-related issues.

Janet had been playing the cello since she was a child and had been playing professionally for quite a few years. She was not a full-time member of the orchestra. Although she worked on a full-time basis, she was a contract employee. This meant that her contract was renewed on a yearly basis. She did not have to try out for her position; the orchestra just had a limited number of full-time cellists.

When I first met with Janet it was the end of her musical season; she had experienced a very trying year and was completely overwhelmed. She started by explaining that she had been very flustered lately. She was even confused about why she was so upset; she said her feelings were all jumbled up inside of her. She was having trouble sleeping, was getting into arguments with her husband, and was having disagreements with her co-workers.

When I said, "Why don't you tell me what is going on?" her

CHAPTER 13

Janet—A Professional Musician

Janet played the cello for one of the local orchestras. She came to see me because she was concerned about her playing. She had been a member of the orchestra for some time now, but thought the quality of her play had been going down lately. Janet was having a lot of anxiety and was experiencing a tremendous amount of stress because of work-related issues.

Janet had been playing the cello since she was a child and had been playing professionally for quite a few years. She was not a full-time member of the orchestra. Although she worked on a full-time basis, she was a contract employee. This meant that her contract was renewed on a yearly basis. She did not have to try out for her position; the orchestra just had a limited number of full-time cellists.

When I first met with Janet it was the end of her musical season; she had experienced a very trying year and was completely overwhelmed. She started by explaining that she had been very flustered lately. She was even confused about why she was so upset; she said her feelings were all jumbled up inside of her. She was having trouble sleeping, was getting into arguments with her husband, and was having disagreements with her co-workers.

When I said, "Why don't you tell me what is going on?" her

reply was, "Oh my, where do I start?" My usual answer is, "Just start anywhere." This may sound a little strange, but over the years I have found clients will prioritize their problems themselves and will start with the most pressing problem.

Janet began with her work. She said the person who played first cello really bothered her this year. Bill had been playing first cello for about five years, but Janet had been with the orchestra much longer than Bill. Now her future was in Bill's hands because if he wanted to, as first cello, he could open up her position for auditions. She would have to fight for her job if this happened and Bill would have a big say as to who would get her position.

Bill had been criticizing her play lately, saying it was not technically correct. No one had ever said this to Janet in the past, so she was concerned the level of her play was actually slipping. Bill had a friend, Bob, who played in Janet's place if she missed a performance. Bill claimed Bob's play was the style he was looking for. He had not actually said this directly to Janet, but had implied it to her and others a few times.

What I often do is try to figure out where a problem started. I feel if I look back on the origin of the problem, both my client and I get a better understanding of the problem. I may ask something like "When is the first time you remember feeling this way?" or I might ask, "When is the first time you were in a situation like this?"

When I asked Janet these questions, she instantly went back to her childhood. She said the first time she remembered having these feelings of inadequacy was when she was around her father. Her father was a very critical man and in his eyes she could do nothing right. He constantly criticized Janet. She said she never got any praise from her father—only less criticism. Her dad was very judgmental and critical about everything she did.

Because her dad was critical anytime Janet tried to do something she developed a fear of doing things. She often would avoid anything that could bring her father's criticism. She said she was never taught how to do things by him, but was expected to be able to do whatever was asked of her. She told me, "I remember being about seven or eight years old, I was out in the garage with my dad, he was hammering something; I asked if I could hammer too. He gave me a spare board, a hammer, and some nails. When I bent the nails, he said, 'What's the matter with you—can't you even hit a nail?'" He never showed her how to hammer a nail; he just criticized her for not being able to hammer properly. Soon she quit asking to help her father.

Where was her mom in all this? Her mom was an alcoholic and although she was around, she was not really "there." Her mom offered Janet a little emotional support. She would say things like, "Don't worry honey, he just had a bad day." Her dad was very critical of her mom as well, so Janet's mom also tried to protect herself from his wrath.

I was curious as to how Janet got into music. My guess was that one would be subject to much criticism while performing. She replied, "My dad knew nothing about music at all, so he was never involved in my playing, therefore he never criticized me."

Janet said she had the same experience playing now that she had as a child around her dad—the fear of being judged. She was scared the conductor, Bill, or someone else would judge her playing and think less of her.

Right away I came up with some steps to try to help her:

Step 1. Recognize her fear of being judged now is actually from the past. The recognition of this would help her understand that the fear is not really tied to what is going on now. Her fears appear real, yet they are tied to the past.

Step 2. Try to tone down her father's and her brother's voice. Both her father and her older brother were very critical of Janet. The internal criticism she heard now was actually the internalized voices of her father and her brother. As I have stated before, if a parent is overly critical of a kid during childhood, the child often internalizes that voice for the rest of his or her life. His or her parents may be dead and gone, but the internal voice will still haunt the person.

Step 3. Internally build up her mom's encouragement. Her mom offered some encouragement, saying, at times, "You can do it." I tried to get Janet to remember this advice and build her mom's voice up. At the same time Janet needed to downplay the bad voices.

Step 4. Get in the moment. I would ask Janet, "What do you think you should do now?" Each time I asked this, she would take a deep breath, exhale slowly, and then start talking. It was clear to me the long slow breath was the answer. She needed to take that deep breath and relax to get into the moment.

Step 5. Use her past successes to help her. Many of the pieces she was playing now, she had played in the past. These were pieces she had played over and over during her years of playing; we needed to get her to use her past successes playing these pieces now. Because of her father's constant criticism, when Janet got through a performance without any major mistakes, she did not see it as a success. She would almost search for mistakes because of her perfectionism that started long ago.

Because of all of these past issues, Janet's confidence never had a chance to grow and develop. It was as if all her life she constantly played in fear. The roots of this fear were back in the original fear of being put down by her father. Here she was, a successful professional musician, yet on the inside she was still a scared little kid.

I think we get into patterns of behavior at an early age. I was trying to get Janet to see she was in a pattern of behavior that was not working for her. I asked, "How is it you have played each of these pieces with few mistakes, for years, yet have very little confidence in your ability?" She was almost dumbfounded when she stopped and thought about this concept. She knew she was capable of playing the music, yet she could not remember a time when she was confident in her playing ability.

She realized when she played, she tried to get through the performance. She never looked back and said to herself, "I did a good job this time." Instead, she would take a deep breath, exhale and think, "Wow, I'm lucky that performance is over—I made it."

Janet was starting to become aware she was evaluating her performance as it was happening. While Janet was playing she constantly worried about making a mistake. If she ever did make a mistake, she would think, "Oh my, I've just ruined the performance." This is like the baseball pitcher who gives up his first hit and thinks, "There goes the no-hitter—I'm in trouble today."

Janet began to realize when she made one mistake—it always led to another and another. Her best performances were the times that for some reason or another, she didn't think about anything and just played.

I worked to get Janet to try not to evaluate her playing during the performance. I suggested she take a few minutes after each performance to review her playing. She could write things down if she felt it would help. She realized that the way she was evaluating her performance now was not working and she was open to try a new way of doing things.

Janet loved to sew. When she was sewing, she was very relaxed and calm; she was able to focus only on sewing. I wanted to tap into this relaxed sewing state and transfer it to a relaxed playing state. With this in mind, I suggested during her performance, she try to get into the same mindset she had while sewing. I wanted her to be focused, yet calm and relaxed. This idea seemed to resonate with her; she agreed to try to put it into practice.

This was a complex task for Janet. Simply identifying that it was her father's voice criticizing her was not enough. It took time for her to realize she did not need to be so self-critical. I tried to get her to see dad's voice with a volume control. When she heard his voice, I asked her to try to lower the volume.

Janet also began to understand her fears about what the other players thought of her were totally unfounded. Janet was often asked to play at other performances outside of her work with the orchestra. One of the most distinguished members of the orchestra asked Janet to play at his daughter's wedding.

We worked on Janet's ability to accept compliments too. One way I did this was to get Janet to note what she did right during her performances. She was so used to focusing on what she did wrong, that if she played a very challenging piece flawlessly, the success would not sink in with her. I had her simply say, "Thank you," when someone complimented her on her performance.

Gradually, things began to change for the better and Janet's playing became more enjoyable for her. Instead of being in constant fear of making a mistake, she was more often able to relax and just play. She was able to tap into the pure joy of playing and her love of music. Janet was finally able to put to rest her father's critical voice.

This whole process took some time, but it worked. Before we met, Janet, like many others, thought, "This is just how I am. I'm critical of myself." When we broke things down, she became aware that this is not how she was, but a result of how her father treated her; the change soon followed.

CHAPTER 14

Gill—A Ten-Year-Old Boy

G ill was ten years old and in the fifth grade. Rarely in my work with athletes do I see someone who is this young. However, Gill's dad felt like Gill needed help now. As a therapist, I do work with kids this age, but often it is for school-related problems.

Gill's mom died when Gill was six years old. She had been sick and in the hospital for close to two years before she died. Gill had very few memories of his mom; he felt an indescribable grief. He was very confused about his emotions. They were all mixed up inside of him. When he did sports he would often have violent outbursts. He would throw bats in baseball, fight kids in other sports, and often yell at referees. His dad was confused and did not know what to do about Gill's behavior. He felt Gill needed therapy and thought with my combination of a sport and therapy background, Gill might open up and talk with me.

When Gill came in, he seemed like a typical ten-year-old boy; he was a bit hesitant for the first few minutes of our first session and then he opened up completely. He began with "Basically, I have no friends," and added, "I never have had any friends." He said kids tease him constantly and he does not know how to handle it. He either fights or cries when teased. If he cries, this leads to more teasing and being called a crybaby. These problems seemed to get worse when last year, in fourth grade, the class went on a field trip to a cemetery.

Gill said he did not cry at his mother's funeral because he was only six years old and did not really understand what was going on at the time. His fourth grade field trip happened to be to the cemetery where his mother was buried. At the cemetery, he broke down and sobbed hysterically. All the emotions he kept locked up inside of him came flooding out. The other kids in the class did not know what to think about his outburst of emotion, not knowing Gill's background.

Because of the incident at the cemetery Gill was being teased and called a crybaby even more often. Gill did not know how to handle these feelings. In Little League he could not control himself and constantly overreacted. If he struck out, he would often cry or throw his bat or helmet. In the field if he made an error he would throw his glove on the ground and have a tantrum. His dad did not know how to deal with Gill's behavior. He was busy working and being a single father.

Gill said he did not keep pictures of his mom around, because if his dad had a woman over, Gill did not want her to think he and his dad were still sad about his mom. He said he did not feel like he knew his mom at all and he wondered what she was like. All he knew was that when she was alive, his parents argued often.

After two sessions with Gill, I met with Hank, Gill's dad. Hank expressed his concerns about Gill. Hank told me not only did Gill's mom die, but both of Gill's grandparents died around the same time. Gill was close to his grandparents and these three losses were overwhelming for both Gill and Hank. Hank said that he and Gill's mother were going to get divorced right before she was diagnosed with cancer, but for medical insurance reasons they stayed together.

Hank also said after his wife died, Gill wanted to sleep in his bed with him. He let Gill do this for a little while, but then told Gill it was time to move back into his own room. Gill would often sleep on the floor and place his body in his room so that his head stuck out into the hallway, so he could see his dad's room.

To try to encourage Gill to behave at school, Hank came up with a reward system. If Gill did not get more than two check marks at school during the week, then they would do something fun on Saturday. Saturday was a fun day for them anyway, but since Hank had started this system two months before, Gill's behavior improved.

I encouraged Hank to talk with Gill about appropriate expressions of anger and suggested they come up with an anger scale from one to ten. On this scale, one would be a little angry and ten would be extremely angry. I felt they needed a scale because Gill always went straight to ten. I suggested that they talk about each level on the scale and the response that would go along with the anger scale. I told Hank that I would work on the scale with Gill in our sessions too.

I suggested Hank try to address Gill's fears of abandonment, because these fears were huge for Gill. With the loss of his mom and his grandparents, Gill feared that his dad might leave too. Gill had told me he was worried his dad might get cancer and die too. Gill was hypervigilant when it came to Hank. If Hank had the flu, Gill thought his dad might die. When Hank was sick, Gill had a hard time concentrating while at school. Hank had two brothers and a sister who lived close by. They had kids and Gill was close to his cousins. I suggested more contact with the cousins, especially since they had lost their grandparents too.

We also went over the concept of consequences. Hank was reluctant to discipline Gill because his mom died. I told Hank he was not to tolerate out-of-control behavior from Gill. We did not need to stop the grief, but we could work to put an end to the throwing of equipment during games. We made a deal that if Gill played a game without throwing anything, Hank would take him for ice cream after the game. The other thing Hank suggested was that if Gill played tantrum-free all week, he and Gill would go see a professional baseball game. Gill loved baseball and this was a great incentive. I know people worry about giving a kid a reward for everything. They wonder if the child will always expect a reward, but in this case I felt like we needed to reward the good behavior, to get rid of the tantrums.

Next we went over what to do if Gill had a tantrum in a game. If he did, he was to spend the rest of the evening with no television, telephone, video games, or Internet access. They would not go to or watch professional baseball together that weekend. If this did not work, Hank was to pull him off the field the instant he had a tantrum. We never had to go to this extreme; with other kids I have gotten to this level, change usually happens quickly, as the kids are embarrassed when their parents pull them off the field.

In the next session I had Gill talk about his mom. He told me all he remembered about her being sick, her treatment, and her death. This was emotional for him and he cried while talking about her. I felt like it was good for him to grieve his mom's death. Since it had happened long ago, in his eyes, he did not need to talk about his feelings. I encouraged him to put up a picture of his mom in his room. He said he would do so and seemed glad to have permission to do this.

Gill and I went over the issues that Hank and I had talked about. Gill seemed to grasp the concept of anger on a scale of one to ten, but he was not sure he could implement the changes in his behavior. We went over what anger at each number would look like. This was enough to get Gill to really try to work on controlling his behavior. I would not be seeing Gill for about five weeks and I felt like we had things in place to help him control his behavior.

In our next session Gill came in and reported his progress, stating he was not crying as much anymore and had made some friends at school. He said, "I must have changed, because I am friendlier now." He said he still had trouble sleeping but that "it has nothing to do with my mom." I thought that perhaps he was reluctant to talk more about his mother because of the intense emotions he expressed in our last session. Surprisingly, he proceeded to talk about his mother the rest of the session.

Gill told me that before his mom died, if she yelled at him, he would take out his aggression in whatever sport he was playing at the time. This is how the pattern developed; he needed a release for his emotions and sports provided that release.

He told me he put a picture up of his mother and would often talk to the picture before going to bed. He would tell her how and what he and his dad were doing. He would also talk about how his games were going and what was going on at school.

Gill reported that his baseball playing was much more controlled and that he was not having tantrums anymore. He and Hank were spending a lot of quality time together. His behavior at school improved too. When his dad picked Gill up from our session, he said "He's doing much better."

Our next session was two weeks later. Gill came in, sat down, and announced, "I don't need a psychiatrist anymore." When I explored the reason for this, after explaining that I am not a psychiatrist, Gill said it was because of money. He said things had been tight for his dad lately and since they are living on one income now, he could not afford to see me. All this information came from a ten-year-old child. Gill was keenly aware of adult problems. He felt he needed to help his dad take care of things around the house, which included saving money. I knew that perhaps Gill was presenting to me that things were great at home so I would agree with him and say that he did not need to see me anymore.

Gill also told me his dad had his girlfriend stay over a couple nights per week. He added, "I know what is going on in there." He said sometimes that he feels like he has to compete with his dad's girlfriend for his dad's attention. When Hank picked Gill up Hank asked if the two of us could meet next time.

Hank came in and said that Gill's behavior was much better and that Gill seemed to be much calmer during baseball games. Gill was now able to handle setbacks with the appropriate amount of anger. The anger scale program was working. Hank wanted to know how to keep Gill's progress going. He was concerned because the anniversary of Gill's mother's death was a couple weeks away. Also, Gill was jealous of his dad's girlfriend. At times Gill would come sit on his dad's lap while he and his girlfriend were watching television.

In the next session with Gill, it was obvious things were not going well for him. He had been getting in trouble at school and almost got sent home from a field trip for acting up. He had also been benched by his baseball coach for out-of-control behavior. When I asked if any of this had anything to do with feelings about his mother and the anniversary of her death, Gill's reply was, "Will you lay off the mother stuff." He then tried to downplay her death and said he needed to move on with his life. I am sure this was not how he felt, but someone probably told him he needed to move on.

Toward the end of our session, Gill began to express concerns about his father's safety. He said if anything happened to his dad, he would end up in a foster home. This was not true, but it provided a lot of insight into Gill's thought process. He said he would make a great effort to not get into trouble anymore.

I ended up having two more sessions with Gill; part of the reason was financial and part of the reason was that summer was approaching and we would both be gone. Mother's Day had just passed and Gill told me he went to the cemetery to visit his mother's grave. He had written her a note and read it at her gravesite. In the note he told her he loved her and missed her. Also, a few days later, when passing the cemetery with a friend, he said, "That's where my mom is buried." After saying this to me Gill looked sullen and confused. When I asked during our session how he was feeling he said, "confused."

As we explored these feelings some more, Gill could see how his mother's death impacted every aspect of his life. When he first came to see me he denied any feelings about her death and he was incredibly volatile, but as we talked more and more about these feelings he became calmer. His behavior both in school and on the baseball field became more even tempered. Gill was gaining more control over his emotions.

I never saw Gill again and could only hope that our work together helped him in the long run and that he lived up to his potential and did not end up a "broken egg."

CHAPTER 15
The Best Sports Has to Offer

O ne of the best examples of what sports have to offer comes from someone most people outside of the
sport of swimming have never heard of—Mark Henderson. Mark swam for us at Cal and was an outstanding collegiate swimmer. Mark took one year off to try to make the 1992
U.S. Olympic team in the 100-meter butterfly. The 100-meter
butterfly is one lap down, a fast turn, and a sprint back in a fifty-
meter pool.

The way things work in swimming is, the top two swimmers
in the finals of the 100-meter butterfly at the U.S. Olympic Trials make the U.S. Olympic team. Even if you get third place at
the Olympic Trials, and have the third fastest time in the world,
you still watch the Olympics on television like everyone else. It
does not matter what your times were earlier in the year or even
in the preliminaries that morning. Everything depends on how
you swim in the final heat at the Olympic Trials.

Mark knew he would have some tough competition to
make the 1992 Olympic team. He would be competing against
Matt Biondi, who won the Silver Medal in the 100-meter butterfly in the 1988 Olympics. Also, Pablo Morales was making a
comeback for the 1992 Olympics after getting third at the 1988
Trials in both the 100-meter and 200-meter butterfly. Pablo was
the world record holder going into the 1988 Olympic Trials in
both the 100-meter and 200-meter butterfly. He did not make
the 1988 Olympic team in either event. Knowing the tough

competition, Mark still took a year off to train for his chance to make his Olympic dreams come true. It seemed he had a good chance to make the Olympic team as Mark was ranked third in the world going into the Olympic Trials.

To qualify to swim at the Olympic Trials one must swim fast enough to reach the very fast qualifying time standards. These time standards are faster than the time standards one must reach to qualify to swim in the NCAA Championships. All who qualify for the Olympic Trials swim in the morning preliminaries. The fastest eight swimmers from the prelims qualify to swim in the final heat that same night. The fastest two swimmers in the finals make the U.S. Olympic team.

In recalling his preliminary swim, Mark told me, "I swam with literally no effort and was just off the American and World Record. I actually backed off at the end of the race! I was out nice and easy and brought the race back strong like I had trained my body to do for the previous four years."

Mark had the fastest time in the prelims, meaning he was seeded first going into the finals. If he could repeat his performance in the finals he would make the Olympic team. However, when Mark saw that he would be swimming in the lane between Matt and Pablo for the finals he changed his strategy. He began to out-think himself. Mark thought he needed to break up Matt and Pablo's race strategy. He knew that Matt and Pablo would expect him to be at their hips at the fifty-meter turn, as Mark was usually not out as fast as everyone else in the first fifty meters of a race was. Mark's strength was in his second fifty meters of the race—he always finished strong. Mark felt if he took the race out fast, and was ahead of Matt and Pablo, he would make them lose their mental focus.

Mark's thinking is an example of a common mistake in sports. People often change what got them there. Many athletes change to a new strategy when their old one worked just fine.

Mark did not tell anyone of his plan. He knows that if he had shared this new strategy with his coach, his coach would have quickly shot down the idea.

In the finals, Mark dove in and took off. By the wall, at the fifty-meter turn, Mark was half a body length ahead of Matt and Pablo. When Mark came up for his first breath after the turn he could hear the massive roar of the crowd. He was ahead of the World Record pace. Mark was out a second and a half faster than he was in the preliminaries. Mentally, he was swimming a totally different race.

Mark kept his lead until the last ten meters, and then he faded to finish in seventh place. Seventh place and his Olympic dreams were shattered. Mark swam his slowest time in years.

Mark was devastated. He had taken a year off to train for this chance and it was now over in less than sixty seconds. What can anyone say to a person in this situation? I went up to Mark, patted him on the back and said, "nice try." It was obvious to me that Mark was in shock. Matt Biondi and Mark are friends. Mark said to Matt, "At least you still have the 50 and 100 free. I'm done."

Mark's thinking is an example of a common mistake in sports. People often change what got them there. Many athletes change to a new strategy when their old one

What makes me say Mark is an example of the best sports has to offer? After the race, Mark stayed up all night talking with his coach and his parents. He explained to them how he had changed his strategy from the prelims to the finals. Ever since he was a young swimmer, Mark tried to learn from his mistakes. His age group coach, Jeff King, from CURL Swim Club trained Mark to come and talk with him after each race. Jeff and Mark would review the race while it was still fresh in their minds. They would always look at ways Mark could improve. While other kids were throwing their goggles, or off sulking by themselves, Mark was figuring out a way to improve. He and Jeff talked after every race—good or bad.

That night at the Olympic Trials, as Mark sat down with his parents and his coach, Rick Curl, they reviewed both the prelim and the final swims. They knew that if Mark had relaxed and swum his own race in the finals, he would have made the Olympic team. Mark was aware of his mistake, but unfortunately in swimming you only get one chance every four years.

The next morning Mark approached Matt and me on the pool deck. Mark asked, "Do you think I should train for Atlanta?" He was talking about the Atlanta Olympics in 1996—four years away. Not many people can set four-year goals and deal with devastating setbacks—Mark could. He had learned from his mistake and was now ready to look forward. This conversation was less than twenty-four hours after he failed to make the 1992 Olympic team.

What happened to Mark? I'll fast forward to 1996. He kept swimming and once again qualified to swim at the Olympic Trials. From 1992 to 1996 he had trained the first half of each season with the distance group. These are the swimmers that swim four- to fifteen-minute races, not fifty-second races, like Mark. Both Mark and distance coach Eran Goral knew that training with the distance swimmers would give Mark the confidence to catch up to anyone the last fifty meters of a race.

After the morning preliminaries in the 1996 U.S. Olympic Trials, Mark was seeded sixth. This is both good and bad. Sixth place means Mark qualified for the finals, however he would need to finish in the top two in the finals that night to make the Olympic team.

Going into the finals Mark would be in the fastest heat of swimmers in the 100-meter butterfly ever assembled—faster than the final heat at the 1992 Olympics. Mark's parents had a huge impact on what happened in the finals. As Mark was getting ready to go to the ready room, his parents said to him, "No matter how you do, know that we love you and had a great time just being here." His parents always gave Mark positive reinforcement and he knew their statement to him was genuine. Mark's parents had made statements like this in the past. Through the years his parents took the time to understand Mark's swimming career. Mark knew his parents' approval of him did not hinge on the results of the finals.

As the swimmers paraded out for the finals, seven of the swimmers were serious and somber knowing the challenge that lay ahead. Mark had a noticeably different approach as he walked toward the starting blocks. He was relaxed, smiling, and talking to people. He stepped up on the starting blocks with the confidence that he would swim his own race this time. He had waited and prepared for this moment for four years—actually his whole life.

As the race started, Mark stayed relaxed and looked straight ahead. At the fifty-meter turn Mark was in eighth place. He stayed calm knowing he could run all the other swimmers down. He accelerated the last fifty meters and began to pass the other swimmers. He finished in second place. Second place and spot on the 1996 Olympic Team! He felt a tremendous sense of pride knowing he attained the goal he set at the same pool four years ago.

At the Olympics in Atlanta, Mark swam the 100-meter butterfly in the preliminaries and finished in ninth place. This means Mark did not qualify to swim in the finals. However, he beat the other American swimmer, which earned Mark a spot on the 4 x 100 Medley Relay. For the medley relay the fastest person from each event qualifies to swim 100 meters of his stroke. The medley relay consists of 100 meters of backstroke, breaststroke, butterfly, and freestyle. Each swimmer starts his leg of the race when the previous swimmer touches the wall.

When the relay came around, for the first time in history, the U.S. team was not favored to win the Gold Medal. The Russians had the World Record holders swimming the butterfly and freestyle legs of their relay. The Russian swimmer had beaten Mark by over a body-length in the 100-meter butterfly. However, as usual, Mark sat down with his coach and watched the video of his preliminary race over and over. They went over corrections Mark needed to make for his leg on the medley relay.

In the finals of the relay Mark swam a great race. He had almost the exact same time as the World Record holder from Russia. They had the two fastest butterfly splits in history. The U.S. team won the Gold Medal and set a World Record. The relay made such an impressive showing that for 1996 the Swimmer of the Year award was not given to an individual, it went to the Olympic Medley Relay Team.

As you look at this part of Mark's swimming career, you see many great things. Without supportive and loving parents Mark would have never experienced this level of success. Mark saw many kids along the way whose parents ran their kids out of the sport. He also had coaches along the way who were concerned with more than just his results. His coaches took the time to nurture Mark and help him focus on how he could improve. He had the perfect combination of support and nurturing from both his parents and coaches.

Mark will admit that he is not the most talented athlete around. But Mark learned how to deal with his setbacks and move forward. It is not the Gold Medal and the World Record that make Mark's story so good. Dealing with setbacks, setting goals, good time management skills, and a healthy self-esteem are what helped Mark. Sure the results were great; they may not always be great. Mark's process was great but more importantly, the process can always be great.

CHAPTER 16

Conclusion

I would like the reader to stop and reflect on the stories in this book. All the individuals I talked about were on the edge. They were at a precarious point in their sports careers and easily could have quit. Most of them continued in their sports and most of them had success. Our work together was a turning point in their careers, and for some, the resulting success in sports was a turning point in their lives. For Paul it was a turning point for the worse. He is probably dead or in jail now instead of living out his NFL dreams.

There are thousands upon thousands of young "eggs" in the same situation as the athletes described in this book. What happens to these kids when they quit sports? Most of the time they end up bitter and angry. They may resent the coach who was verbally abusive toward them. I have had clients tell me they still are angry, many years later, with their high school coach, because the coach shamed them. The coach put them down in front of others and told them they didn't have what it takes to make it. Some coaches told the athletes they were weak. The implication of this type of verbal abuse on young and emotionally developing young kids is tremendous. Many coaches fail to realize that yelling at athletes does not make them mentally tough. **The cornerstone of mental toughness is self-confidence.** Coaches and parents should work to help young athletes become more confident in themselves.

When kids quit because their parents pushed them, they

may resent their parents. Often this resentment lasts a lifetime! This is outrageous. People spend their lives trying to live up to their parents' expectations. This desire to please often lasts long after their parents are dead and gone. Since they were never good enough, in their parents' eyes, they never feel good enough about themselves. Because their parents pressured them, they in turn treat their kids the same way, creating a vicious cycle.

Sometimes kids quit because they were teased by their teammates. They end up bitter and resent their former teammates for bringing an end to their careers, many times before they even got started. They often go through life feeling "less than." This bitterness and resentment comes out in work, school, and in their relationships.

When kids who quit sports become adults they often push their own children to excel, which is detrimental to their children's emotional well-being. People who did not have a fulfilling sport experience also may turn into weekend warriors. They become those who injure themselves sliding into second base in a recreational softball game. Because their sport experience was unrewarding and unfulfilling, they play with a level of intensity that is uncalled for in a fun game. Emergency rooms across the country are constantly dealing with people who are in their thirties, forties, and fifties who have injured themselves playing in fun games with friends.

Many children are being pushed in sports so hard at such a young age that they are getting serious injuries. Ask any pediatrician about the rise in the incidence of sports injuries in young children. What you will find is many kids are hurting knees, shoulders, ankles, and elbows at a young and tender age. Kids are suffering muscle strains, pulls, and tears from overuse. Many young athletes are turning to performance enhancing drugs to help them succeed in sports. These young athletes think performance enhancing drugs will bring instant success. Some parents even encourage the use of these drugs. Both parents and children fail to take a long-term look at the young athlete's life. Some college basketball coaches encourage recruits to look at a fifty-year plan. Many young basketball players simply wanted to play in the NBA; they think no further than a few years ahead. Playing in the NBA is a great goal, but having a fifty-year plan ensures success for life. Performance enhancing drugs do not fit into a fifty-year plan. However, a rewarding sports experience lasts for life.

Some of those who do not have a rewarding sports experience become fanatical fans for professional sports teams. It is my guess many of these people are frustrated with their own lack of success in sports. In turn, they try to live through whatever professional team is successful. They probably also push their own kids to succeed where they failed in sports. This produces a horrible cycle that unfortunately can go on for generations. It is time to bring an end to this cycle.

You can bring an end to this cycle by starting with your family and your children. Treat your children like the precious treasures that they are. Help nurture and guide them through their sports experience. It is my view that there is no experience that can be as rewarding as a good sports experience. Make sure your kids have a great experience; this is your responsibility, not the child's.

If you coach, start with your team and your league. The professional teams are not coming to hire you away from your Little League team. You are there to help teach, guide, and nurture kids, so go back to having fun. As a coach you should have two simple goals. First, teach your athletes the proper technique in the sport that you coach. Second, produce confident athletes. Self-confidence is the key to success in sports; a coach can play a huge role in the development of an athlete's self-confidence.

If coaches and parents can keep the focus on proper instruction and having fun for young kids, the sports experience will be wonderful. As I have stated before, the definition of fun changes over time. It is much more fun and meaningful for individuals to succeed in sports when they are eighteen or twenty years old than it is for them to succeed when they are ten or twelve years old. We must develop a long-term perspective to help young kids get all the potential benefits from their sports experience.

In my experience some athletes are artists. Their athletic performances are an artistic expression of what is inside of them. Matt Biondi was truly an artist in the swimming pool. Fortunately, through a long and productive career, Matt was able to express his inner artistic/athletic ability. I have a quote on my wall that reads:

"If you bring forth what is within you, what you bring forth will save you. If you do not bring forth what is within you, what you do not bring forth will destroy you."*

Too many kids are not able to bring forth what is within them because they are driven out of sports at a young age. For these young athletes, being unable to express their inner athletic/artistic ability leads to pain and frustration for the rest of their lives.

Compared to a lifetime, any sports career is short lived. A rewarding career in sports is a wonderful experience for those who can, at the end of their careers, look back on their time in sports with a sense of integrity, fulfillment, and self-satisfaction. The physical and psychological benefits from "optimizing the sports experience" can last a lifetime. However, the actual results are not nearly as important as the experience itself. In whatever capacity you work with kids, remember that our children are a rare and precious commodity. Treasure them and do your best so they do not become "broken eggs."

---

* Jesus. *The Gospel of Thomas; Gnostic Gospels*

Sources

1. *Alcoholics Anonymous*. Alcoholics Anonymous World Services, 1939.

2. Andersen, Mark. *Doing Sport Psychology*. Champaign, Ill.: Human Kinetics, 2000

3. Basch, Michael Franz. *Doing Psychotherapy*. New York: Basic Books, 1980

4. Beck, Charlotte Joko. *Everyday Zen: Love and Work*. San Francisco: Harper, 1989

5. Beck, Charlotte Joko. *Nothing Special: Living Zen*. San Francisco: Harper, 1993

6. Brenner, Charles, MD. *An Elementary Textbook of Psychoanalysis*. New York: Anchor Books, 1974

7. Coon, Dennis. *Introduction to Psychology: Exploration and Application*. Belmont, Calif.: Brooks/Cole, 1998

8. Frankl, Viktor E. *Man's Search for Meaning*. New York: Washington Square Press, 1959

9. Freud, Anna. *The Ego and the Mechanisms of Defense*. Guilford, Conn.: International Universities Press, 1946

10. Fromm-Reichmann, Frieda. *Principles of Intensive Psychotherapy*. Chicago: University of Chicago Press, 1960

11. Glenmullen, Joseph, MD. *Prozac Backlash*. New York: Simon and Schuster, 2000

12. Gorski, Terrence T. and Merlene Miller. *Staying Sober*. Independence, Mo.: Herald House/Independence Press, 1986

13. Hanh, Thich Nhat. *Living Buddha, Living Christ*. New York: Riverhead Books, 1995

14. Jewell, L. N. *Psychology and Effective Behavior*. St. Paul, Minn.: West Publishing, 1989

15. Jones, Ernest. *The Life Work of Sigmund Freud; Volumes 1, 2, 3*. New York: Basic Books, 1953

16. Kahn, Michael. *Between Therapist and Client : The New Relationship*. New York: W. H. Freeman and Company, 1991

17. Kubler-Ross, Elisabeth. *On Death and Dying*. New York: Macmillan Publishing, 1969

18. *Living Sober*. Alcoholics Anonymous World Services, 1975

19. Maltz, Maxwell, MD. *Psycho-Cybernetics*. Englewood Cliffs, N.J.: Prentice Hall, 1960

20. Nideffer, Robert. *The Inner Athlete*. New York: Ty Crowell, 1976

21. Reynolds, Bill. *Cousy: His Life, Career and the Birth of Big Time Basketball*. New York: Simon and Schuster, 2005

22. Rogers, Carl R. *On Becoming a Person*. Boston: Houghton Mifflin, 1961

23. Sarason, Irwin G., and Sarason, Barbara R. *Abnormal Psychology: The Problem of Maladaptive Behavior*. Englewood Cliffs, N.J.: Prentice Hall, 1999, 2002

24. Sokolove, Michael. *The Ticket Out: Darryl Strawberry and the Boys of Crenshaw*. New York: Simon and Schuster, 2004

25. Tutko, Thomas, PhD. *Sports Psyching*. New York: Tarcher/Putnam Books, 1976

26. *Twelve Steps and Twelve Traditions*. Alcoholics Anonymous World Services, 1952

27. Wooden, John R. *My Personal Best*. New York: McGraw-Hill, 2004

28. Wooden, John R. *They Call Me Coach*. New York: McGraw-Hill, 1988

29. Yee, Rodney. *Yoga: The Poetry of the Body*. New York: St. Martins, 2002

Index

Acknowledgments

This book was written with much help. First of all, I must thank my daughter Ashton, my initial editor. Fortunately, I have a daughter who is an English major. I thank her not only for what she added to this book, but also for keeping some of the crazy ideas that I had out of this book.

Every two weeks since 1990, I have dinner with a friend, John Hammerman. John's advice was very helpful in many aspects of this book. Since 2000, Mike Madigan has joined us. Mike is a former English professor who spent many hours editing this book. He helped me reword sentences to make the book flow much better. Mike's help was awesome!

My fellow Chabot College professor Ken Williams gave me incredible feedback. Ken edited the whole book in one weekend; thanks Ken.

Jeff Greenwald is a former graduate student of mine who now has his own practice as a psychotherapist. Jeff made the video *Fearless Tennis* and gave me very good feedback for this book.

Thanks to all my graduate students at John F. Kennedy University, who over the years have helped me clarify many of the ideas presented in this book.

In many of the examples in this book I have altered some facts to preserve anonymity when necessary. I would like to thank my former clients, especially those of you who allowed me to include our work together at the risk of others identifying you. You know who you are.

I owe tremendous thanks to Nort Thornton and the University of California Men's Swim Team. My experience at Cal was invaluable. While coaching at Cal I was fortunate enough to come in contact with people like Matt Biondi, Mark Henderson, Roque Santos, Sean Killion, and many other great people, who were also great swimmers.

I would like to thank Matt Biondi for the foreword to this book. We share many memories together. I appreciate Matt taking time from his busy schedule to help with this book.

I want to thank both Sean Killion and Mark Henderson for sharing their experiences with me.

Thanks to Jeremy Solomon at Inkwater Press for publishing this book. Also my editor at Inkwater Press Linda Weinerman did a fantastic job editing this text.

Although my grandmother, Florence G. Johnson, has been dead since 1996, I want to acknowledge her for the tremendous impact she has had on me. Finally, I would like to thank my mother, Jean C. Morin, for all her love and support over the years.

About the Author

Tom Morin, MFT (Marriage Family Therapist), is a psychotherapist in private practice in Oakland and Marin County, California. He teaches Intro to Psychology and Abnormal Psychology at Chabot College in Hayward, California. He is also teaches a Counseling Skills class in the Sport Psychology Program at John F. Kennedy's Graduate School of Psychology in Pleasant Hill, California. Tom is on the staff at MPI, a chemical dependency treatment program in Oakland, California. A former swim coach, Tom was Matt Biondi's personal coach for the 1992 Olympic Games.